Mountains are massive and  but hopeful. Dr. Engle leads shows us how God calls us to worship on his holy mountain. From the garden to the New Jerusalem, we are shown the centrality of God in worship and how this can enhance our present earthly worship.

—**Dominic A. Aquila**, President, New Geneva Theological Seminary

Bible readers are mountain climbers, because the biblical authors and poets often invite us to meet the Lord in high places. Engle takes us to a series of summits and uses lively prose to recreate these high-elevation revelations. What is more, he demonstrates how these mountaintop experiences motivate and direct our worshipful response.

—**John A. Beck**, Adjunct Faculty, Jerusalem University College; Author, *Along the Road* and *The Holy Land for Christian Travelers*

Dr. Paul Engle provides a much-needed resource to the church in his book *When God Draws Near*. The book clearly unfolds not only who the covenant God is but also how he wants his people to worship him in his presence. I wish that this book had been available to me when I started out as a pastor forty years ago.

—**Bruce Cresswell**, Associate Pastor of Senior Adults and Visitation, Christ Covenant Church, Matthews, North Carolina

Engle focuses the heart of biblical worship on the presence of God dwelling with his people. . . . His final two chapters, on the Mount of Olives and Mount Zion above, are especially moving and motivating for the church today as we participate in heavenly worship through Christ by faith. . . . A great resource for teachers and learners in the educational ministry of the local church.

—**Mark Dalbey**, President and Associate Professor of Applied Theology, Covenant Theological Seminary

Worship has been Paul Engle's lifelong pursuit—in his own spiritual life as well as through his teaching, preaching, and writing. . . . Each of [these] seven summits . . . offers a unique high vantage point from which we can view worship. Engle's own experiences climbing these mountains brings immediacy to his wise insights.

—**Lee Eclov**, Senior Pastor, Village Church of Lincolnshire, Lake Forest, Illinois; Author, *Feels Like Home*

This insightful and helpful book can serve as a handbook for worshippers . . . to teach them what it means to gather for worship and the impact that worship can have on their lives. . . . Paul Engle takes readers on a biblical journey of mountaintop worship that enables them to see what God is doing in them and among them as they worship—as they meet the God of the universe and experience his presence.

—**Scott M. Gibson**, Professor of Preaching and David E. Garland Chair of Preaching, Baylor University's Truett Seminary

A timeless and refreshing mountain-climbing guide that provides an illuminating perspective on what worship is. . . . Summons us to delight in the vistas that worship creates by pondering what worship is.

—**Darwin K. Glassford**, Executive Pastor, Harderwyk Ministries, Holland, Michigan

Does your heart long for deep, meaningful worship? Do you wish that God himself had given us a blueprint for worship? *When God Draws Near* shows how he has done just that! Herein Dr. Paul E. Engle provides a biblical theology of worship from Genesis to Revelation, taking the reader from Eden to the heavenly Jerusalem. If you desire God-centered, soul-satisfying worship, this is your book!

—**Timothy K. Hoke**, Acting Vice Chancellor, African Bible University

Theologically rich, engaging to read, and filled with unexpected implications, Paul's book will energize us as we weekly climb Mount Zion in the heavenly Jerusalem to join the myriad of angels and those who have gone before us in praising our ascended King Jesus.

—**Robert D. Jones**, Associate Professor of Biblical Counseling, The Southern Baptist Theological Seminary; Author, *Pursuing Peace* and *Uprooting Anger*

If our chief purpose is to "glorify God and enjoy him forever," then no other activity is as important to the believer's well-being as worship. . . . Paul Engle describes the biblical and theological terrain that shapes this spiritual landscape. Thoughtful and engaging, this book will transform your understanding of what it means to approach God.

—**John Koessler**, Faculty Emeritus, Moody Bible Institute; Author, *Practicing the Present*

Interesting biblical information . . . enriched by the personal experiences the author gained while traveling in the Middle East and elsewhere. The author adds layer upon layer of insight into the images and theology of worship, filling the word *worship* with meaning and motivating the reader to delight in our calling to be worshippers. I heartily recommend the book.

—**Craig Brian Larson**, Editor, The Preacher's Toolbox series; Blogger, *Knowing God and His Ways*

Dr. Paul Engle is a master teacher. I have been the beneficiary of his teaching ministry many times. Paul provides compelling insights about the subject he treasures the most: the worship of our great God. I am grateful that he has chosen to make the profoundly insightful discoveries he has acquired through his extensive travels and studies accessible in book form.

—**Bernie Lawrence**, Senior Associate Pastor, Christ Covenant Church, Matthews, North Carolina

Today's church is both divided and confused about worship. Our focus is too often on satisfying human needs rather than on offering praise to our eternal God. Paul Engle uses the stories of seven mountains in Scripture to remind us . . . what worship is all about.

—**Douglas J. Moo**, Wessner Chair of Biblical Studies, Wheaton College; Chair, Committee on Bible Translation

Engle is a captivating tour guide who leads his readers through hiking expeditions to seven mountains . . . proving foundational to a biblical understanding of worship. Engle is also a riveting storyteller who weaves his firsthand accounts of climbing these mountains together with significant truths about worship. The result is an utterly fascinating and interesting read.

—**Rory Noland**, Director, Heart of the Artist Ministries; Author, *Worship on Earth as It Is in Heaven*

Dr. Engle confronts the global crisis of man-centered worship and its tendency to dominate the evangelical church. . . . This book insightfully takes us on an exciting journey of redemptive-history "mountaintops" in order to reclaim God-centered, biblical worship and bring us *Coram Deo!*

—**Bob Penhearow**, Founder, Senior Lecturer, Carey International University of Theology; Editor, *Systematics for God's Glory*

An imaginative journey through the Bible that is organized around visits to seven of its best-known mountains as a way of showing the true nature of worship. Because worship is central to Christian life, a book like this, in which the author has dug deeply into Scripture, is most welcome.

—**David F. Wells**, Distinguished Senior Research Professor, Gordon-Conwell Theological Seminary

What an intriguing and readable book on worship geography! Whether or not your worship this Lord's Day felt like a mountaintop experience, Paul Engle uses the mountains of the Bible to explain what happens when Christians gather for worship—and how we might do it better.

—**Michael Wittmer**, Professor of Systematic and Historical Theology and Director of the Center for Christian Worldview, Cornerstone University

WHEN
GOD
DRAWS
NEAR

Also by Paul E. Engle

The Baker Funeral Handbook
The Baker Wedding Handbook
Baker's Worship Handbook
Discovering the Fullness of Worship
God's Answers for Life's Needs
The Governor Drove Us Up the Wall: A Guide to Nehemiah
Guarding and Growing: A Study in 2 Peter
Worship Planbook: A Manual for Worship Leaders

WHEN GOD DRAWS NEAR

Exploring Worship
from Seven Summits

Paul E. Engle

P&R
PUBLISHING
P.O. BOX 817 • PHILLIPSBURG • NEW JERSEY 08865-0817

Library of Congress Cataloging-in-Publication Data

Names: Engle, Paul E., author.
Title: When God draws near : exploring worship from seven summits / Paul E. Engle.
Description: Phillipsburg : P&R Publishing, 2019.
Identifiers: LCCN 2019021171 | ISBN 9781629955971 (pbk.) | ISBN 9781629955988 (epub) | ISBN 9781629955995 (mobi)
Subjects: LCSH: Worship. | Worship--Biblical teaching.
Classification: LCC BV10.3 .E54 2019 | DDC 264--dc23
LC record available at https://lccn.loc.gov/2019021171

To my wife, Margie,

for reasons that would fill a million pages . . .

CONTENTS

ILLUSTRATIONS

PREFACE

Not long ago, I spent an entire week in Seattle, Washington, without once seeing the sun. Undaunted by the drizzle, fog, and unremitting thick gray clouds, I kept sneaking glances toward the southeast horizon, hoping to catch a glimpse of the nearby snowcapped Mount Rainier—the topographically prominent stratovolcano that usually dominates the landscape. But to my disappointment, the summit remained totally obscured for the entire week.

When at last I returned to the airport, I consoled myself with the thought that there would be future business trips to the Pacific Northwest and perhaps a future sighting of Mount Rainier. Exhausted from the long, sun-deprived week and longing to get home, I buckled up in my window seat. As the plane climbed upward, I peered out the window at the dark clouds that had surrounded me all week long.

Until, all of a sudden, there it was! We had broken through the clouds. The eastern horizon lit up with a luminescent pink and yellow glow. Projecting through and above the clouds, the snow-covered Mount Rainier pointed up 14,411 feet toward its Creator. Below its peak was a surrounding blanket of billowing clouds that extended for miles and captured the radiance of the morning sunrise. The majestic mountain had been there all week long; I just hadn't seen it.

My experience can serve as a paradigm for what happens in

the case of all too many people who attend corporate worship services each Sunday. Clouds and fog can obscure what is happening in the invisible, spiritual realm when believers enter a service. This book is written to awaken Christians to biblical realities that take place in worship assemblies but that often go unnoticed.

In the following pages, we will break through the clouds in order to survey the horizon from several mountaintops—not Mount Rainier, but seven summits from the Bible. Over the course of the book, we'll travel to Mount Sinai, then Mount Zion in Jerusalem, then Mount Carmel, then Mount Gerizim in Samaria, then Mount Hermon in northern Israel, and then the Mount of Olives. Finally, we will make the ultimate climb to the heavenly Mount Zion. Together we'll discover, from the recorded events that took place on each of these sites, God's design and purpose for worship. By the time you arrive at the last chapter, you will have journeyed from Genesis and creation all the way to Revelation and consummation.

For decades, I have had the privilege of teaching pastors and church leaders on the subject of worship in the United States as well as in many other countries. I owe much to thousands of pastors and students whose feedback has helped me to further refine the insights the Lord has taught me through my study of Scripture. I have ingested countless books on the theology of worship. The teaching and writing that I have done on this subject have been enriched by several trips to Israel, where I have explored the biblical summits and archaeological sites I describe here.

In one of his books on worship, A. W. Tozer wrote, "This book is a small attempt to fan the flame of holy desire toward God. I hope you will catch the passion and press forward to delight in the conscious, manifest presence of God."[1] This reflects the beat

---

1. A. W. Tozer, *Experiencing the Presence of God*, comp. and ed. James L. Snyder (2010; repr., Minneapolis: Bethany House, 2014), 26.

of my heart for this book also. I have provided diagrams, charts, and maps for illustration throughout. If you wish to use this book in a class or a small group setting, each chapter concludes with questions for discussion and reflection.

The experience of Sunday corporate-worship assemblies is "the most outward, Godward hour in our weeks. . . . It's a time when the invisible is made visible: the scattered church comes together; the signs of the kingdom are present in bread and wine and in the waters of baptism. The gathered church is a foretaste of the new heaven and the new earth."[2] My prayer is that the journey we take in this book will elevate our perspectives and open our spiritual eyes to new realities so that we come to joyfully anticipate Sunday worship as the highlight of each week.

Maranatha! Let's begin.

Paul E. Engle

---

2. Mike Cosper, *Recapturing the Wonder: Transcendent Faith in a Disenchanted World* (Downers Grove, IL: IVP Books, 2017), 29.

Part 1

GETTING READY FOR THE CLIMB

1

UMBRELLA NEEDED

Beginnings of
Edenic Worship

The Presence of God in our midst—bringing a sense of
godly fear and reverence—this is largely missing today.
You cannot induce it by soft organ music and light
streaming through beautifully designed windows.
—A. W. Tozer, *Whatever Happened to Worship?*

A young boy sat next to his mother in a Sunday morning church service. He was restless and bored stiff. His mom had insisted that he leave his Nintendo at home lest he be distracted or, worse yet, irritate the people sitting behind him. Suddenly the boy's wandering eyes spotted a bronze plaque on the side wall of the church that showed letters, stars, and the outline of a flag. "What's that?" he asked his mother, and she whispered in reply, "Oh, those are the names of people from our church who died in the service." There was a long pause, as the boy was obviously upset with that answer. Panicking, he nudged his mother again. "Mom, Mom—did they die in the first or the second service?"

I recognize that story is not likely to cause you to roll in the aisles with laughter. It might even elicit a groan. But I tell it because it makes a point.

To all too many people, a worship service is boring—something to be endured until they exit the church building and life goes back to normal. Perhaps this is part of the reason why there has been much experimentation in corporate worship in North America during the past couple of decades. In an attempt to connect with people, many churches have made seismic changes in how they conduct Sunday morning worship. Perhaps more changes have been made in the structure, style, and format of worship services in the last twenty years than in the past two hundred years combined.

A few years ago, the wife of a well-known megachurch pastor and popular author offered a controversial view of the goal of worship. A YouTube video, which is now removed and unavailable, showed her making the following statement before an overflow crowd of worshippers in their arena-like meeting place: "When you come to church, when you worship him, you're not doing it for God really. You're doing it for yourself!"

I suspect that many would take exception to this human-centered view of worship and might blink in incredulity. "Did I hear her correctly?"

Why Bother?

Why should you take the time and exert the energy to explore the subject of worship? Is it really that important to devote a whole book to this subject? Allow me to highlight several reasons why I believe that the central gathering of the church in worship is indispensable to a healthy Christian life.

- *You and I have been summoned.* Sunday worship fulfills Scripture's clear command that we meet together on the

18

first day of each week. Our Lord actively looks for our worship. "True worshipers will worship the Father in the Spirit and in truth, for they are the kind of worshipers the Father seeks" (John 4:23). Amazing. The Father *seeks* your worship and mine. Let us draw near.

- *The experience of corporate worship shapes and reflects our view of God.* It's the setting in which our appetite for God and our understanding of his acts and attributes are stimulated and stretched.

- *Sunday worship is the best way to prepare for what will engage us for eternity.* William Nicholls wisely asserts that "worship is the supreme and only indispensable activity of the Christian Church. It alone will endure . . . into heaven, when all other activities of the Church will have passed away."[1]

Many churches engage in worthwhile activities such as counseling ministries, food banks for the hungry, marriage-preparation training, evangelistic outreaches, and many others you could likely name from your own church. Yet in the new heaven and earth, these programs and ministries will be unnecessary and will fade away. The one activity that will not disappear is worship. That's how important it is to get it correct, here and now, in preparation for what's coming. Our focus on worship in this life will reap eternal dividends.

I have long been captivated by a claim that author and Cambridge scholar C. S. Lewis made: "If I find in myself a desire which no experience in this world can satisfy, the most probable explanation is that I was made for another world."[2] Or, as Ecclesiastes 3:11 expresses it, "He has also set eternity in the

---

1. William Nicholls, *Jacob's Ladder: The Meaning of Worship* (repr., Richmond: John Knox, 1963), 94.

2. C. S. Lewis, *Mere Christianity* (New York: Macmillan, 1952), 106.

human heart." You and I long for a way to connect with the eternal world. To explore the dimension[3] of worship is to satisfy that longing.

Overarching Umbrella

Far too many people approach worship without an umbrella, and that's exactly what I hope to provide in this book.

What do I mean? I'm referring to an overarching theme or metanarrative that ties Scripture together—that extends from eternity past to eternity future—arching from Genesis to Revelation. And what is that big-picture umbrella that helps us make

Fig. 1.1. Umbrella: God's Plan to Dwell with Us

3. When I apply the word *dimension* to worship, I use it to refer to the invisible atmosphere, sphere, or reality that we enter when we gather with other believers in the name of Christ on the first day of the week.

sense of worship? It's this dominant theme: "the presence of God" (or, in Latin, *Coram Deo*)—God's plan to dwell with his people.

You may be thinking, What's the big deal here? Isn't "presence of God" just another one of those obvious evangelical clichés? Isn't it just another buzzword that we hear in prayers, sing in the lyrics of Christian songs, and read on PowerPoint slides? No—a thousand times no. We need to dig deeper.

The theme of divine presence is a bright thread that is woven through the entire Bible. It's a beautiful melody that plays from Genesis to Revelation for those who have ears tuned to hear. Like mountain peaks rising above the mist, the stories from Genesis to Revelation provide us with elevated views of the divine presence.

The place to begin an examination of worship is not the book of Acts, as some would suppose, but rather the book of Genesis and the earliest experience of worship. Our setting is the garden of Eden.

Worship before the Fall in the Edenic Garden

In eternity past, out of darkness and emptiness, a personal God chose to speak and to bring the world into ordered being. God created Adam and Eve in his image and gave them the capacity to know and worship him. Just as plants in the garden needed sunlight in order to flourish, so humans would not flourish without spending time in the light of God's presence. God situated Adam and Eve in a perfect garden that was a sacred place or temple filled with his presence. Some scholars have concluded that the garden was located on a mountain. "The elevated location of the garden of Eden is indicated by the fact that a single river flows out of Eden, before dividing to become four rivers."[4] The prophet Ezekiel

---

4. T. Desmond Alexander, *The City of God and the Goal of Creation* (Wheaton, IL: Crossway, 2018), 62; see also Genesis 2:10–14.

reinforces this idea by referring to "Eden, the garden of God" on "the holy mount of God" (28:13–14). The Greek Old Testament describes the garden's geographical area with the word *paradeisos*—a term used to describe an enclosed garden or walled park. My wife and I have always enjoyed being together, walking and talking—especially at the end of a long day. Our neighborhood is blessed with an abundance of brilliant-colored Knock Out roses, crepe myrtle trees, camellia bushes, and *Clematis* vines that climb up mailbox posts, trellises, gas lantern posts, and everything vertical. We sometimes imagine what Adam and Eve experienced in their tropical paradise as they walked and talked with their transcendent creator God. Worship for them was natural and immediate. Communion was pure and open. Original worship, prior to the fall, was not hindered by the barrier of sin.

What was God's plan for Adam and Eve? "God blessed them and said to them, 'Be fruitful and increase in number; fill the earth and subdue it'" (Gen. 1:28). From the start, God planned to expand the original garden of Eden beyond its borders. His plan was that the whole earth would become a dwelling place for his descendants. But something went horribly wrong. The expansion of Edenic perfection never happened.

Effects of the Fall on Worship

The story is a familiar one. God commanded Adam to fast from one tree in order that he might feast at the other trees and enjoy communion with his Creator.[5] But Adam and Eve deliberately disobeyed God—with dire consequences. The fellowship between God and his creatures was ruptured. "Then the man and

5. See Jonathan Gibson, "Worship: On Earth as It Is in Heaven," in *Reformation Worship: Liturgies from the Past for the Present*, ed. Jonathan Gibson and Mark Earngey (Greensboro, NC: New Growth Press, 2018), 4. A helpful discussion of worship in Eden can be found from pages 2–8.

his wife heard the sound of the LORD God as he was walking in the garden in the cool of the day, and they hid from the LORD God among the trees of the garden" (Gen. 3:8). Instead of choosing to obey and worship God, Adam and Eve chose to hide from his presence. From that moment on, their worship of God was no longer pure and undefiled.

How did things change after the fall? In lots of ways. For starters, God pronounced a triple curse on his creation (see Gen. 3:14–19):

- *The curse of the ground.* The growth of thorns and thistles would necessitate hard work on Adam's part in order for him to produce food for his family. Thus, Adam's mission to expand the borders of Eden geographically was made more difficult. His environment became his enemy. From here on out, cultivation of the land would be toilsome for him—and for us. Sore backs and blistered hands are a continual reminder to farmers and gardeners that we live on a fallen planet.
- *The curse of generation.* Labor pains would accompany the birth process for Eve and for subsequent generations. The mission to fill the earth would be difficult.
- *The curse of separation.* Adam and Eve were expelled from the garden and from its immediacy of worship. Author Greg Beale explains that "God's presence in his dwelling place satiates our longings for relationship, satisfaction and significance, and the opening chapters of Genesis show how God intended those longings to be properly satisfied—in Eden."[6] But now things would move in a new direction.

6. G. K. Beale and Mitchell Kim, *God Dwells among Us: Expanding Eden to the Ends of the Earth* (Downers Grove, IL: InterVarsity Press, 2014), 17.

God's Ultimate Plan to
Restore the Temple of Eden

Adam and Eve had succumbed to the Serpent's temptation and eaten the forbidden fruit, so God not only confronted the couple but also addressed the serpent, saying, "I will put enmity between you and the woman, and between your offspring and hers; he will crush your head, and you will strike his heel" (Gen. 3:15). In this *protoevangelium*—the first hint of the gospel of redemption—God pointed to his plan to send Christ, who would break down the barriers that hinder sinful humans from entering the presence of a holy God in worship. This promised future Redeemer would be called "'Immanuel' (which means 'God with us')" (Matt. 1:23).

Fig. 1.2. Umbrella: God's Plan to Restore His Unmediated Presence

Though all human efforts to achieve utopia have ended in failure, the gospel brings hope. When we come to the book of Revelation, we discover that one day God will remove the curse and eternally restore his unmediated presence. He will usher us into the heavenly city/garden that will mirror and reflect the garden of Eden. Read this wonderful promise: "I heard a loud voice from the throne saying, 'Look! God's dwelling place is now among . . . his people, and God himself will be with them and be their God'" (Rev. 21:3).

Notice the clear parallels between Genesis 1–3 and Revelation 21–22. God's dwelling presence bookends the story of the Bible.

Garden of Eden Worship (small plot in Middle East)	Heavenly Jerusalem Worship (all the new earth)
Creation of the sun and moon (Gen. 1:14–18)	Removal of the unnecessary sun and moon (Rev. 21:23)
Creation of day and night (Gen. 1:3–5)	End of nighttime (Rev. 21:25; 22:5)
River watering the garden (Gen. 2:10)	River of life flowing from the throne (Rev. 21:6, 22:1, 17)
Tree of life (Gen. 2:9)	Tree of life (Rev. 22:2)
Precious stones (Ezek. 28:13–14)	Precious stones (Rev. 21:18–21)
Cherubim guarding the entrance to the Garden (Gen. 3:24)	Cherubim surrounding the throne and worshipping God (Ps. 80:1; 99:1; Isa. 37:16)
Experience of God's immediate presence for Adam and Eve (Gen. 3:8)	Enhanced experience of God's eternal presence for all the redeemed sons of Adam and daughters of Eve (Rev. 21:3)

God created us to dwell with him—to satisfy ourselves with his divine presence, which will one day fill the entire new earth and heaven. In our present state, however, we are given only small, incomplete, imperfect glimpses of this future reality when we gather for worship on the first day of each week.

Pollster George Barna asked people whether they feel a real and personal connection with God when they attend services. He reported that over a third of church-attending Americans never experience God's presence in worship services—they don't connect.[7] Let me raise some questions for you to ponder: How would you explain this disconnect? How can worship services be planned to make Christians more aware of the divine presence? How can we avoid anything in our worship that would distract people from its God-centered focus?

Unicorn in Narnia

C. S. Lewis understood the biblical vision of worship, and in his classic series of fantasy novels, The Chronicles of Narnia, he artfully used his imagination to help us to picture the fulfillment of the trajectory of God's promise to dwell with us his people. In the final book in the series, *The Last Battle*, Lewis describes how the Unicorn enters a deeper country, at the creation of a new Narnia, and sums up what everyone around him is feeling. He cries out, "I have come home at last! This is my real country!

---

7. See "What People Experience in Churches," Barna, January 8, 2012, https://www.barna.com/research/what-people-experience-in-churches/.

A similar poll by the Pew Research Center found that 37% of adults under age 30 do *not* feel a sense of God's presence in worship services. However, a higher percentage of women, older adults, and non-college-educated people reported that they *do* sense God's presence in services. See "Why Americans Go (and Don't Go) to Religious Services," Pew Research Center, August 1, 2018, http://www.pewforum.org/2018/08/01/why-americans-go-to-religious-services/.

I belong here. This is the land I have been looking for all my life, though I never knew it till now."[8]

For Lewis, the hope of our Christianity is about returning home to where we really belong. It's about finally achieving our dream of returning to the garden. In our present worship, we enjoy a small foretaste of what awaits.

At age sixty-seven, Alexander Graham Bell, inventor of the telephone and holder of thirty patents, was asked to deliver the graduation address at Sidwell Friends School in Washington. The graduates were surprised to hear the brilliant Scottish-born scientist confess that he struggled with inattentiveness. He had recently taken a walk around his family's long-held property in Nova Scotia. He was intimately familiar with the terrain—or so he thought. With stunned disbelief, however, he discovered a moss-covered valley that led to the sea. It had been there all along! Bell told the graduates, "We are all too much inclined to walk through life with our eyes shut. There are things all round us and right at our very feet that we have never seen, because we have never really looked."[9] A similar phenomenon may occur in our worship services today. Some of us have attended church for years. We've sung the songs, read the Scriptures, mouthed the responses, and yet missed much of what's occurring in the invisible dimension. Open our eyes, Lord.

It is my prayer that what you read here will open within you new dimensions of appreciation for worship.

8. C. S. Lewis, *The Last Battle*, in *The Chronicles of Narnia* (New York: HarperCollins, 2004), 760.
9. Quoted in Amy E. Herman, *Visual Intelligence: Sharpen Your Perception, Change Your Life* (Boston: Houghton Mifflin Harcourt, 2016), 14–15.

27

Questions for Reflection and Discussion

1. From your experience or observation, explain why some people are bored with corporate worship services. What are some solutions to this?
2. Why is it worthwhile to spend time focusing on worship and growing in our understanding of it?
3. What are some effects that the human fall into sin, in Genesis 3, had on worship?
4. Why do you think some people have a longing to get back to the garden? Can you think of some echoes of Eden that occur down through history, even to today? Describe God's plan to deal with this Edenic garden longing that people feel.
5. How would you describe some of the parallels between Genesis 1–3 and Revelation 21–22?
6. The pollster George Barna reports that a significant percentage of church attenders never experience God's presence in worship services. What do you think accounts for this? Is the root cause related to the planning and content of services, or does the problem simply rest with individual church attenders? Is it possible to be a church attender without being a worshipper?
7. What insight does C. S. Lewis provide in *The Last Battle* that helps us to understand worship?

2

THE MOUNTAINS
ARE CALLING

The Significance of Summits in Worship

The concept of God living on a holy mountain is a significant
theme in the Old Testament. However, this same theme
frames the entire Bible. It begins with the garden of Eden
in Genesis and ends with New Jerusalem in Revelation.
—T. Desmond Alexander, *The City of*
God and the Goal of Creation

We expected that this would be the trip of a lifetime—and it did
not disappoint. My wife and I gritted our teeth, gripped the door
handles of our safari van for dear life, and pretended not to mind
the layer of dust that was coating us and everything around us. We
were determined to take it all in: the orange soil landscape, the
emaciated cattle, the lean-to roadside stands, and the seemingly
endless stream of Kenyans who walked along the side of the road
in colorful garb—some precariously balancing heavy loads on
their heads and others carrying bright yellow jugs of water home
to their families.

After several hours of bumpy roads, we were jolted out of our seats as our guide brought the vehicle to an abrupt stop in the middle of nowhere. He pointed to the sight I had waited decades to see. "There it is. Wow," he exclaimed; "we can see it today—Mount Kilimanjaro. You're lucky it's clear enough to see!"

I had to pinch myself as I gazed across the distant Tanzanian border at the glaciated terrain of a mountain. It seemed almost surreal. "I'm actually here!" The hazy August heat waves of the equatorial plains did not dampen my enthusiasm. This was the roof of Africa—the climbing goal of more than 25,000 adventure-seekers each year. No digital camera could begin to capture the wonder of this landscape that had held thousands of stories for generations.

Mountains in the Land of the Bible

In the weeks before I sighted Kilimanjaro, I had been teaching African pastors and students in two different institutions about the treasures of corporate worship. One of the dominant metaphors I employed was that of mountains. On an earlier hiking experience that had involved some of the more prominent mountains in Israel, I had begun to realize several important connections between mountains and worship that merited further reflection.

The Bible refers to mountains about five hundred times. This is not surprising, because mountains dominate the landscape of Israel. Almost everywhere in the country, there are mountains on the horizon. It's little wonder that the Jewish leader Joshua used mountain ridges as natural boundaries when he divided the promised land among the twelve tribes. Throughout biblical history, people viewed mountains as gifts God had given to help them provide for their daily needs. Crops were planted and sheep were led to graze on hillsides and mountains. High mountain ridges provided viewing platforms and signaling stations when foreign

The Seven Summits

In 1980, American businessman Richard Bass not only decided to climb Mount Kilimanjaro—the highest peak in Africa, at 19,340 feet—but also determined to climb the highest peaks on each of earth's seven continents: Asia's Mount Everest, North America's Denali, South America's Aconcagua, Europe's Mount Elbrus, Australia's Mount Kosciuszko, and Antarctica's Vinson Massif, as well as Africa's Kilimanjaro. Within five years he had reached his goal, thus launching a new wave of competition among mountaineers from around the world who wanted to imitate Bass and accomplish his same goal. To date, more than 350 people have successfully climbed what are called the Seven Summits.

Continent	Summit	Country	Altitude
Africa	Kilimanjaro	Tanzania	19,340 ft.
Antarctica	Vinson Massif	Antarctica	16,050 ft.
Asia	Everest	Nepal and China	29,035 ft.
Australia	Mount Kosciuszko	Australia	7,310 ft.
Europe	Mount Elbrus	Russia	18,510 ft.
North America	Denali	United States	20,310 ft.
South America	Aconcagua	Argentina	22,841 ft.

armies approached. Mountain clefts and caves provided refuge during military attacks.

But there's something even more significant about mountains in Scripture. "Mountains and hills are a master image of the Bible, through which one can trace the whole course of biblical history and doctrine in microcosm."[1] To trained eyes, geography is a map that helps us to understand theology. This is especially true when it comes to understanding the biblical theology of worship.

Mountains as Places of Spiritual Significance

The religious or spiritual significance of mountains appears prominently in Scripture. Ancient people living in the land of the Bible often sensed a closeness to God and a feeling of transcendence when standing on a mountaintop. Perhaps this is a reflection of God's general revelation at work in people who are created in his image. Throughout history, this awareness has continued to take place—especially among mountaineers and monks. The eighteenth-century Disentian monk Placidus a Spescha regularly climbed to the summit of one of the mountains near his monastery in the Swiss Alps. He would sleep there, wrapped in his cowl and habit, in order to draw closer to God. More recently, Maurice Herzog led a group of French climbers on an expedition in the Himalayas that reached a peak of over eight thousand meters. He described his thoughts upon reaching the summit this way: "I was consciously grateful to the mountains for being so beautiful for me that day, and as awed by their silence as if I had been in church."[2] An intriguing choice of words.

In the days of the ancient Canaanites, it was not uncommon for shrines and high places that were dedicated to the worship of pagan gods to be located on mountains. Temples to Baal were

1. Leland Ryken, James C. Wilhoit, and Tremper Longman III, gen. eds., *Dictionary of Biblical Imagery* (Downers Grove, IL: InterVarsity Press, 1998), s.v. "mountains."

2. Maurice Herzog, *Annapurna*, trans. Nea Morin and Janet Adam Smith (New York: Dutton, 1952), quoted in Robert Macfarlane, *Mountains of the Mind: Adventures in Reaching the Summit* (2003; repr., New York: Vintage Books, 2004), 8.

built on the tops of mountains. Ancient people viewed mountains as magical places that their gods actually inhabited.

Even to this day, on another continent, the Bakonjo tribe in southwest Uganda believe that the jagged peaks of the Rwenzori Mountains are the home of a deity called Kitasamba. Some have reported that tribal elders would walk the circumference of the mountain range once a year, offering sacrifices in return for protection. Similarly, the Kikuyu and Maasai tribes in Kenya believe that the upper reaches of Mount Kenya are the home of their supreme god Ngai.

Now contrast these superstitious views of individual pagan gods with the view of God that was held by the Israelites and revealed in Scripture. The Israelites understood that the true Creator of the universe lived in heaven and had never been confined to one particular mountain. Yet God did occasionally appear on a mountaintop in order to make himself known, and many of the most significant events in the life of Christ also took place on mountains. In the Old Testament, mountains often became the locations for giving and renewing divine covenants, as well as locations for worship.

Perhaps you have heard the phrase "thin place" or "thin space" used to describe mountaintops. Yes, the air is thin when you climb to high altitudes, but I'm using *thin* in another sense. There's a Celtic saying that heaven and earth are only three feet apart and that, in thin places, the distance is even smaller. The Celts believed that people experience God more readily—with more immediacy and intimacy—when that separating veil is thin. The Celtic Christians taught that the distance between God and man collapses as one senses the presence of God. Mountains have often been treated as thin places that lead to a heightened awareness of God's holy presence.

C. S. Lewis reminds us, most notably in his Narnia tales, that scenes of nature such as towering mountains frequently inspire us to worship. Nature often invokes feelings of grandeur, sublimity, and majesty that deeply move us. Lewis believed that such feelings are not merely subjective and personal—that there is something objectively and inherently majestic about mountains. As one Lewis scholar observed, "The beauty of the mountain is telling you that a greater beauty exists above it. The mountain is only an image—a shadow—pointing to that greater reality. That greater reality is the true reality that is the source of all beauty and the spring of all joy and delight that spills over into nature. That reality is God himself."[3]

New Testament scholar and defender of orthodoxy J. Gresham Machen spoke often of his deep love for mountains. He achieved his goal of climbing one of the most famous mountains in the world—the Matterhorn in Switzerland—and later wrote, "I shall never forget those last few breathless steps when I realized that only a few feet of easy snow separated me from the summit of the Matterhorn. When I stood there at last—the place where more than any other place on earth I had hoped all my life that I might stand—I was afraid I was going to break down and weep for joy."[4] Indeed, mountains have a way of turning our thoughts godward in joyful worship.

What Mountains Teach Us about God's Attributes

Mountains can further stimulate our worship by giving us glimpses of the attributes of our creator God.[5] Their massive size

3. Thomas Williams, *The Heart of the Chronicles of Narnia: Knowing God Here by Finding Him There* (Nashville: W Publishing Group, 2005), 31–32.

4. J. Gresham Machen, "Mountains and Why We Love Them," *Christianity Today* 5, no. 3 (August 1934), available online at https://opc.org/machen/mountains.html.

5. A helpful article on mountains is "Mountain," in *Zondervan Dictionary of*

speaks to the power and greatness of the One who created them. The Creator can weigh mountains, shake them, crumble them, and melt them like wax if he chooses. One author sagely remarked, "People in the post-modern world have forgotten the austere and unaccommodating landscapes of the mountain—[they] need to recall again the smallness of self and the majesty of [God.]"[6]

You may have sung the classic Isaac Watts hymn that begins, "I sing the mighty power of God, that made the mountains rise."[7] Perhaps Watts was reflecting the inspired words of David that refer to God as the one "who formed the mountains by [his] power" (Ps. 65:6). The prophet Isaiah tells us that God "weighed the mountains on the scales and the hills in a balance" (40:12). You and I have no cause to be fearful even if, as Psalm 46:2 posits, "the mountains fall into the heart of the sea." Why? Because our God is bigger than the splash they would cause!

The stability of mountains also reminds us of God's steadfast love for us: "'Though the mountains be shaken and the hills be removed, yet my unfailing love for you will not be shaken nor my covenant of peace be removed,' says the LORD, who has compassion on you" (Isa. 54:10).

Mountains likewise remind us of the eternal nature of the kingdom of God. Most of the mountains in the central zone of the land of the Bible are composed of hard limestone that erodes at the rate of only one imperceptible centimeter every thousand years. Mountain peaks give the impression of enduring forever. But the love and righteousness of God on which we depend are even more enduring than hard limestone. "Your righteousness is like the highest mountains" (Ps. 36:6). "Before the mountains

---

Biblical Imagery, gen. ed. John A. Beck (Grand Rapids: Zondervan Academic, 2011), 177–79.

6. Belden C. Lane, *The Solace of Fierce Landscapes: Exploring Desert and Mountain Spirituality* (New York: Oxford University Press, 1998), 53.

7. Isaac Watts, "I Sing the Mighty Power of God," 1715.

were born or you brought forth the whole world, from everlasting to everlasting you are God" (Ps. 90:2).

In today's world of sensory overload, you don't need to be a news junkie in order to realize that earthly kingdoms come and go—that nations rise and fall, sometimes overnight. Yet the good news is that there exists an eternal kingdom of God that will both destroy and outlast them all. The prophet Daniel saw a vision from God that explained the dream of the king Nebuchadnezzar, who had seen a statue of gold, silver, bronze, iron, and clay. In the vision, Daniel sees a kingdom pictured as a great rock, which "struck the statue [and] became a huge mountain and filled the whole earth" (Dan. 2:35). Daniel goes on to explain,

> In the time of those kings, the God of heaven will set up a king-dom that will never be destroyed, nor will it be left to another people. It will crush all those kingdoms and bring them to an end, but it will itself endure forever. This is the meaning of the vision of the rock cut out of a mountain, but not by human hands—a rock that broke the iron, the bronze, the clay, the silver and the gold to pieces. (vv. 44–45)

Mountains have always served as showcases of the eternal nature of their Creator.

Seven Summits of Worship

As we scan the horizon of Scripture, seven key mountains on the biblical landscape stand out in terms of their importance in worship. We will climb them not based on their geographical location but rather in the chronological, historical order of their appearance in the biblical story of worship. The view from these seven summits will challenge us to understand more fully what worship is all about.

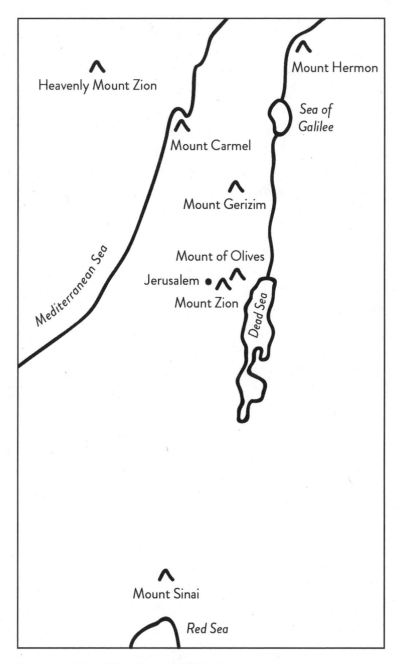

Fig. 2.1. Map: The Seven Biblical Summits

Yes, the climb will take time and energy, but it will be worth it. As we look at the view from these mountaintops, we'll gain insights that will enrich our understanding and experience of worship for a long time to come. We'll encounter the presence of God atop each. We'll visit some historic "thin places" and recall what occurred at each site. You might say that mountains are defined as much by the stories attached to them as by their size and shape. The stories associated with these seven mountains, which are linked by the overarching metaphorical umbrella, form a unified picture of what transpires when God's people assemble to worship.

So, my fellow mountain-climber, are you ready? I trust that, by God's grace and with his help, this will be a mountaintop experience—a "thin place"—for both of us. Whatever you do, don't get stuck in the misty lowlands. Don't settle for the easy path through the valley. Let's exercise our worshipping muscles and climb to new heights. As William Blake wrote, "Great things are done when men and mountains meet."[8]

Questions for Reflection and Discussion

1. Why do you think the Bible refers to mountains so frequently?
2. Contrast the views of mountains held by worshippers of pagan gods with the view held by the Israelites in the Old Testament.
3. Explain the term "thin place" as it applies to mountains. Have you ever had any "thin place" experiences?
4. What do mountains convey to us about the attributes of God?

8. William Blake, "Gnomic Verses," in Northrop Frye, ed., *The Poetry of William Blake* (New York: Random House, 1953), 79.

5. What are some of the summits in the Old and New Testaments that became places for worship?
6. What insight does C. S. Lewis provide about the beauty of mountains?
7. What do you hope will happen in your life as a result of this study of worship?

Part 2

CLIMBING SUMMITS IN THE OLD COVENANT

3

OFF TO THE RIGHT START

> ## Mount Sinai: Mountain
> ## of Assembled Worship

Worship is drawing near to the Holy One; his presence effects
a sense of solemn joy, and of densely humbling awe. It is
this that creates our overwhelming sense of privilege that he
welcomes us into his presence. For worship involves first and
foremost God's welcome of us, not our welcome of each other.
—Sinclair B. Ferguson, in *Reformation Worship*

All the Seven Wonders of the Ancient World have disappeared except for one: the Great Pyramid of Giza. A couple of years ago, people around the world were asked to vote online for what they thought should be the "New Seven Wonders of the World." Yes, I took the opportunity to be one of the more than a hundred million voters, and I am happy to report that my choice—Machu Picchu, the lost city of the Incas—made it to the final list.

My fascination with Machu Picchu peaked several years ago when my wife and I visited Peru. My wife and I cheated and took the easy way up, catching a blue PeruRail train early one chilly morning to travel into the mountains. Once we arrived at the station nearest to the mountain, we began the climb of a lifetime. Steep, uneven steps that were combined with high altitude (7,970 feet above sea level) added to the challenge—but also to our overwhelming sense of accomplishment when we arrived at the summit.

In awed silence, we marveled at the remains of the civilization that were in full view before us. Archaeologists have identified the ruins of several temples at this sacred site: the Main Temple, the Temple of Condor, the Temple of the Three Winds, and the Temple of the Sun. The latter was erected by the early Incas as a site where they could honor and make ritual offerings to the ancient Incan sun god, Inti.

While exploring the temple ruins, we were startled to see a man with a full beard and a long, flowing white gown appear out of nowhere. He stood rigidly in front of us. It was a bit creepy, and my wife darted off in another direction to avoid an encounter. I quickly reminded myself, "No, this is not Moses, and I'm not on Sinai."

The mountain we will focus on in this chapter did not make it into the New Seven Wonders of the World. Nor is it considered a safe site for tourists to visit in the current political climate. This mountain, however, is far more significant to our study of worship than Machu Picchu.

God Chose an Awesome Location to Reveal His Presence

The opening two verses of Exodus 19 begin the front-page story of an event that occurred at Mount Sinai three months after God's people fled from Egypt. Having barely escaped the pursuing chariots of Pharaoh's soldiers, the people began their trek across the barren land known as the Sinai Peninsula. You have probably seen that triangular peninsula on the maps at the back of your Bible. Its rugged, rocky, moon-like landscape juts out into what is today called the Persian Gulf.

Under Moses's leadership, the Israelites traveled to the town of Rephidim in the southern Sinai. They continued on through this largely uninhabited territory until they arrived at the foot of Mount Sinai on a spring day in late May or early June. It was at this mountain that God would reveal his divine presence among his people.

Why This Time and This Place?

Why might God have chosen this exact time and particular location of Mount Sinai to meet with his people?

His timing was critical, and it represents an important turning point in the history of his people. The encounter could not have taken place while the people were living under the conditions of oppressive slavery in Egypt and unable to leave. Nor could it wait much longer, because God's people were about to embark on a trek into the promised land. It was critical that they be equipped for the journey. They needed to be taught God's laws, and they also required instructions on how to build the tabernacle—a portable tent that would travel with them to their divinely appointed worship locations. This was a strategic time for God to appear before his people.

He may have chosen this location because the dominating mountain peaks of the region symbolically put mere mortals in their place. While living in Egypt, some Israelites may have traveled along the Nile River and marveled at the great pyramids. From personal experience, I can vouch that when you stand at the base of the pyramids in Giza, you are overwhelmed with your own insignificance. That hardly compares with how the Israelites must have felt while standing at the base of these mountains in the Sinai Peninsula. They would have been overwhelmed with their own smallness and humbled to receive a message from God, the Creator of those ancient mountains.

Mount Sinai Today

Numerous scholars have tried to locate Mount Sinai, which has resulted in as many as a dozen theories about where it was situated. Since the fourth century, the traditional site for Mount Sinai has been a peak that is also known as the Mountain of Moses. In fact, as early as the fourth century, Helena, mother of the Roman emperor Constantine, arranged for a church to be built on this mountain's summit. In 1859, the scholar Constantin von Tischendorf found one of the oldest and most famous early manuscripts of the Bible on the Mountain of Moses—what has come to be called Codex Sinaiticus, which is now housed in the British Library in London but was made available on the internet in 2008.

The Mountain of Moses is an impressive, high mountain— 7,497 feet above sea level—almost the same height as Machu Picchu. More than three thousand steps make it an exhausting, two- to three-hour climb for physically fit visitors. Adjacent to this mountain is a flat plain that spans over four hundred acres. Why is this important? Because the Israelites, who numbered at least six hundred thousand men plus women and children at that time, needed an area of land that was large enough for them to spread out their tents while they camped for ten to eleven months before moving on in their journey to the promised land.

Several years ago, while studying in Jerusalem, I was determined to visit Mount Sinai, having been denied access to it on an earlier attempt. But, to my great disappointment, my contacts in Jerusalem strongly advised me against making an excursion into this volatile desert region. Safety issues related to terrorist activity and recent kidnappings were a major concern, and they remain concerns to this day.

Josephus, the first-century Jewish historian, described Mount Sinai as being "the highest of all the mountains that are in that country," "very difficult to be ascended by men" due to its height and sharp cliffs, and impossible to look at "without pain of the eyes." But, beyond all this, he wrote that "it was terrible and inaccessible, on account of the rumour that passed about, that God dwelt there."[1] Awesome!

Finally, the lack of rain and other natural resources around Sinai meant that the Israelites were forced to turn to God for their very survival. An annual rainfall that struggles to reach even one inch means sparse vegetation. You might say that this setting helped God to shape a receptive audience. For many months, the people would stay at the base of Mount Sinai—completely dependent on the Lord.

God's Presence Revealed through a Covenantal Relationship

Moses experienced a private audience with God on Mount Sinai. Their conversation (see Ex. 19:3–8), which established the covenantal relationship between God and his people, took a form that was familiar in the Near East during that era: a suzerainty treaty.

A suzerainty treaty was a document that spelled out the arrangements or covenant agreed on by two or more parties. Often it was an agreement between a great king and his vassals, which followed a recognizable pattern of preamble, historical prologue, stipulations, and blessings. Archaeologists have uncovered examples of these treaties that date to the second millennium before Christ—the time when the biblical Israelites entered into a covenant with God at Sinai.

1. Josephus, *Antiquities* Vol. 2, Book 3, chap. 5.1, in *The Works of Josephus: Complete and Unabridged*, new updated ed., trans. William Whiston (Peabody, MA: Hendrickson Publishers, 1987).

Preamble

God's personal covenant with his people begins with a preamble. The Lord summons Moses and instructs him on how he is to convey the terms of the covenant to the people of Israel: "This is what you are to say to the descendants of Jacob and what you are to tell the people of Israel" (Ex. 19:3).

Historical Prologue

The prologue gives the historical background of the relationship between God and his people. God wanted his people to recall, and never forget, how he had made his presence known to them in the past by sending the plagues, defeating the armies of Pharaoh, and leading the people through the wilderness to Mount Sinai. God used a vivid metaphor to describe what he had done for them: "I carried you on eagles' wings and brought you to myself." (v. 4) Picture a giant eagle, with widespread wings, swooping under her eaglet who is just learning to fly. What a poignant picture of the Lord's tender care over his people as they would set out from the mountain and head into unknown territory. It's the same vivid imagery that is used in the song of Moses later on: God protected his people "like an eagle that stirs up its nest and hovers over its young, that spreads its wings to catch them and carries them aloft" (Deut. 32:11).

When we are confronted with the uncertainties of the future, Scripture reassures us of God's commitment to be present with us always. Perhaps the next time you sense a need for God's comforting presence, you might also consider the promise of Isaiah 40:30–31:

> Even youths grow tired and weary,
>   and young men stumble and fall;
> but those who hope in the LORD
>   will renew their strength.

They will soar on wings like eagles;
> they will run and not grow weary,
> they will walk and not be faint.

How could you not want to worship such a God of love?

The Story of Eric Liddell

These familiar verses from Isaiah aptly describe the life of the Scottish athlete Eric Liddell, who won an Olympic gold medal at the 1924 summer Olympics in Paris for the men's four hundred meter race—a feat that is celebrated in the award-winning film *Chariots of Fire*. Following his Olympic success, Eric Liddell surprised and disappointed many people when he boarded a ship to China after sensing a call from God to serve as a missionary. Extreme hardships followed, including imprisonment in a Japanese prison camp, where Eric died of a brain tumor at the young age of forty-three.

In 2007, someone happened on Eric's simple grave in China, and a tombstone was erected with this fitting inscription: "They shall mount up with wings as eagles. They shall run and not be weary." The same God who had carried the Israelites to the promised land on eagles' wings had likewise carried Eric through his travels and testings.

Stipulations

God next specifies the terms of the covenant he is making with his people. "Now if you obey me fully and keep my covenant, then out of all nations you will be my treasured possession" (Ex. 19:5). This is staggering. God says that he considers his people to be his own treasure. How unlike the imagined and often feared pagan and tribal deities who were believed to inhabit remote mountains in many locations around the world. He is the God of all nations—the ruler of the universe—who in a personal way proclaims that he has singled out his people as his treasured possession.

The good news is that this covenant relationship between God and his people is not restricted to ancient Israel. God's people failed to keep the covenant that called them to be God's treasured possession—but Christ didn't fail in his calling. So now through Jesus we, the true Israel, are God's special possession. The Bible often repeats the covenantal theme that God will be our God and that we will be his people. Peter picks up this thought when he says that those who are part of the church are "God's special possession" (1 Peter 2:9). "The people of God are a treasure-people, a people for God's own possession. The relationship that defines the church is this relationship of possession by God."[2] Again we must ask ourselves, how can we not want to worship that kind of God?

Blessings

The next section of the covenant includes some blessings: "'Although the whole earth is mine, you will be for me a kingdom of priests and a holy nation.' These are the words you are to speak to the Israelites" (Ex. 19:5–6). Here we see that the Israelites were not only God's treasured possession but also a kingdom of priests. It was God's plan that the whole nation should mediate God's grace to the nations of the earth. This would fulfill the covenant promise God had made with Abraham, in which he promised that through him all nations of the earth would be blessed.

There's more. Not only are the Israelites told that they are a treasured possession and a kingdom of priests, but they're also told that they are a holy nation. Again, Peter uses these same terms to describe those of us who are members of the church: "You are

---

2. Edmund Clowney, *The Doctrine of the Church* (Nutley, NJ: Presbyterian and Reformed, 1969), 11.

a chosen people, a royal priesthood, a holy nation, God's special possession, that you may declare the praises of him who called you out of darkness into his wonderful light. Once you were not a people, but now you are the people of God; once you had not received mercy, but now you have received mercy" (1 Peter 2:9–10). No wonder God expects us to give him worship. That's what declaring his praises is all about. Each time you and I gather in our churches to pray and sing his praises, we acknowledge that we are in covenant relationship with him. We are blessed indeed, and so we in turn bless him. Worship becomes a time of covenant renewal.

After receiving this divine covenant, Moses descended the mountain and shared the news of the covenant with the people. With one voice they responded, "'We will do everything the LORD has said.' So Moses brought their answer back to the LORD" (Ex. 19:8). To be sure, this was not a breezy or dismissive answer on the part of the people. God had done a work in their hearts, and they strongly affirmed their intention to obey him completely.

Fast-forward forty years. This time it's Joshua, not Moses, who is standing before the Israelites and challenging God's people as they prepare to enter the promised land. We once again hear the people cry out, "We will serve the LORD. . . . We will serve the LORD our God and obey him" (Josh. 24:21, 24). How encouraging this must have been for Joshua—as it continues to be for believers today, when successive generations affirm their faith and express their desire to live a life in obedience to God.

God Chose to Awesomely Descend before His People

Let's go back to the Mount Sinai assembly. God had just given a covenant that Moses in turn had conveyed to the nation, and the people had responded wholeheartedly with a promise to obey God. Anticipation built as God prepared to meet his people.

53

Perhaps you are wondering, why the need for such an appearance? Isn't God omnipresent? Yes, he is ontologically omnipresent, in terms of his essential being and existence. Omnipresence is an important divine attribute. Yet the omnipresent God can and sometimes does choose to go beyond and to manifest his presence in unique ways on special occasions—often in theophanies. This is what God's people were about to witness at Mount Sinai.

The Lord gave Moses advance warning about what was about to happen and why: "I am going to come to you in a dense cloud, so that the people will hear me speaking with you and will always put their trust in you" (Ex. 19:9). Although he was physically invisible, God's voice would be audible to the people. He would be surrounded by a dark cloud that would envelop the mountain. No doubt God wanted the people to know that Moses was the designated leader who had been divinely chosen for them—the one whom they should follow from that point on. Moses had the blessing of God himself.

God is totally holy, and his people are sinful. Thus, careful preparations had to be made before the people were allowed to enter his awesome presence (see vv. 10–15). First, the people had to wash their clothes—a symbolic action of cleansing that was indicative of an inner heart attitude. Their clean clothes reflected their purity of heart in their desire to approach a transcendently holy God.

Second, God told the people that during this three-day preparation period they must refrain from sexual relations as husbands and wives. This is not in any way implying that marital sex is sinful. Quite the opposite. The Lord wanted the people to be free from distraction and to focus on the awesomeness of coming into his presence. This calls to mind Paul's counsel in 1 Corinthians 7:5: "Do not deprive each other except perhaps by mutual consent and for a time, so that you may devote yourselves to prayer. Then come together again so that Satan will not tempt you because of your lack of self-control."

A commentator explains the Exodus passage this way: "There are special occasions of prayerful preparation and worshipful activity that call for avoidance of the usual, nonsinful personal indulgences and demand special, focused, self-denying attention to God. The common denominator is prayer: close focus upon God requires both time in prayer . . . and an attitude of special attention to God (coming as clean and well dressed as one would in the case of appearing before anyone he or she wanted to honor) as well as a denial of things that focus on the self so that one can focus on God."[3]

Third, God required the people to stay off the mountain because it was holy ground. Moses was allowed to climb to the top, and the seventy elders could come partway, but the people were not permitted to cross the boundaries and had to remain below. "Be careful that you do not approach the mountain or touch the foot of it. Whoever touches the mountain is to be put to death" (Ex. 19:12). No one should dare to enter the presence of the Holy One recklessly or casually—a salutary reminder for today's worshippers as well.

As the story moves on, we see that the people readily complied with the preparations for worship that God requested. And then it happened—God broke through with cosmic phenomena in verses 16–25. The Lord could just as easily have conveyed a verbal message to Moses and left it at that. But instead, what came next was unforgettable! A total sensory experience unfolded. The air exploded with flashes of lightning and bolts of thunder. A thick, ominous cloud descended over the mountain and enveloped them. The people soon smelled smoke. Flames of fire

---

3. Douglas K. Stuart, *Exodus*, The New American Commentary 2 (Nashville: B&H Publishing, 2006), 426.

appeared atop the mountain while the ground trembled underneath their feet.

Some skeptics have proposed that the commotion and pyrotechnics may simply have been a volcanic eruption. Really? This is hardly believable in light of the fact that the phenomena were precisely timed to occur on the third day after the people had made careful preparations and were waiting at the foot of the mountain. Without a doubt, this was a divinely orchestrated theophany.

What Is a *Theophany*?

The word *theophany* comes from two Greek words: the term for "God" (*theos*) and the word for "appearing" (*phaino*). It is used to describe an appearance of God that is tangible to the senses. "Theophany represents an intensive form of the presence of God. So theophany is like a subtheme within the broad theme of God's presence."* Throughout the Old Testament, God's presence is commonly portrayed in conjunction with storm imagery.

* Vern S. Poythress, *Theophany: A Biblical Theology of God's Appearing* (Wheaton, IL: Crossway, 2018), 29.

The meaning of this theophany became clearer when suddenly, above the sound of thunder, a piercing trumpet blast was heard. This likely came from a curved ram's horn, which was called a *shofar*. The noise from the trumpet became louder and louder as the Lord drew closer and closer. God was on the move. The sound seemed to be coming from the thick cloud and billowing smoke that enveloped the mountain. The phenomena that the people were experiencing served as a dramatic announcement of the divine presence of the God of the universe. Beyond any doubt, the Lord himself was descending onto the summit of Mount Sinai.

The real climax came when the people heard the voice of God himself. This was holy ground. The atmosphere was electric

---

Shofar, So Good

Tourist shops in the Old City of Jerusalem sell imitations of the ancient shofar today. I know from experience that it is impossible to play a tune of multiple notes on one, having purchased a small shofar in the Old City of Jerusalem and struggled to make noise from it. I confess to having fun taking it into the classroom and using it as a teaching resource. If I handed my shofar to you and you put it to your lips, you might produce a single high note and perhaps a single low note, but not much else. The shofar is still used today in Jewish holiday celebrations and can be seen and heard on YouTube videos—just in case you're interested.

**Fig. 3.1.
Shofar**

---

with the presence of God. Little wonder that the people trembled! Some years later, Moses recalled this gathering at Sinai: "Remember the day you stood before the LORD your God at Horeb, when he said to me, 'Assemble the people before me to hear my words'" (Deut. 4:10). Four other times in Deuteronomy this mountain event is called an *assembly*.[4]

A Prototype Assembly

The Hebrew word for "assembly" is *qahal*. In the Greek translation of the Old Testament, the Septuagint, the equivalent word is *ecclesia*, which is also used in the New Testament for the church. It's logical to conclude from the translation of these Hebrew and Greek words that the church has always been an "assembly of

---

4. See 5:22: "your whole assembly there on the mountain"; 9:10: "the day of the assembly"; 10:4: "the day of the assembly"; 18:16: "the day of the assembly."

God"—that is, people who gather in the presence of God for the purpose of worship. What sets the assembly of the church apart from political assemblies, school assemblies, sports assemblies, music concerts, and any other gathering of people? It's a special revealing and awareness of God's presence (not simply his universal omnipresence) as he chooses to make himself known.

This assembly at the foot of Mount Sinai was a *prototype assembly*—a forerunner, a precursor, a model. It was a primitive or early form of assembly in which God revealed to his people his design for the church. It was always his plan that the church consist of people who uniquely belong to God through Christ. God's people, then and now, gather in assembly each Lord's Day for the purpose of entering the presence of God in worship. We do this in anticipation of what God has planned for our future.

Can you guess where I'm going with this? At Mount Sinai, fire and trumpet fanfare announced the coming of God. One day, trumpets will sound again when Christ returns in the clouds to assemble all his saints for the ultimate eternal festival of praise. First Thessalonians 4:16 assures us that one day we will hear with our own ears "the trumpet call of God." Second Thessalonians 1:7 tells us that "the Lord Jesus [will be] revealed from heaven in blazing fire with his powerful angels." This imagery recalls Sinai.

Looking back, we now understand that Sinai was an early prototype of the ultimate future assembly of worship that will take place when Jesus Christ returns and Eden is restored. Scripture promises that "he comes to be glorified in his holy people and to be marveled at among all those who have believed" (2 Thess. 1:10). You and I should be asking ourselves if we are ready for the sound of the trumpet. Every time we assemble for corporate worship, we are engaged in preparation. We assemble each Lord's Day to enter the presence of God, looking back on the past but anticipating the future. Maranatha! Even so, come quickly, Lord Jesus!

Are you bored with worship? Grasping the invisible reality of what God intends for his people will go a long way toward eliminating even fleeting apathy or boredom. After all, we are standing on holy ground.

In the following chapter, we will linger at Mount Sinai in order to take a closer look. Perhaps you will discover new realities that will expand your appreciation of worship the next time you attend a service.

Questions for Reflection and Discussion

1. What is the traditional site of Mount Sinai, and why do many scholars (although certainly not all) place it at this location?
2. Describe the pattern that was followed by the Sinaitic covenant that God entered into with his people.
3. What is the significance of God's instructions for how the people were to prepare to meet with him? Do you think this has any implications for us today?
4. What elements did God use to convey the majesty of his presence at Mount Sinai?
5. What does it mean to say that this event was a prototype assembly?
6. Summarize the lessons that are taught in Exodus 19 and their application to our assemblies of worship. How can we use these in our churches, while recognizing the similarities and differences between the Sinai assembly and our present assemblies of worship?
7. How does inattention affect people in worship services? What can be done to overcome it? How can we encourage people to view worship as an appointment to meet with God?

4

A TENT BETWEEN
TWO MOUNTAINS

Interlude: Tabernacle Worship

*The triune God is the only thing large enough and
interesting enough to bear the weight of glory, and
ultimately worship. Anything else will break your heart.*
—Matt Papa, *Look and Live*

Camping is not everyone's idea of a dream vacation. My childhood memories of digging trenches in the pouring rain around
our family's hand-me-down canvas tent, and of waking up during
a thunderstorm to find myself lying in a soaking-wet sleeping
bag, no doubt contribute to my own negative attitude about it.
Camping seems to be one of those experiences that people either
relish or avoid at all costs.

For God's ancient people, tenting was not an option but a
way of life. Their location at the base of Mount Sinai, where we
left off in the last chapter, proved to be a divinely chosen camping
ground. It was here that the people experienced the prototype
worship assembly, as God appeared amidst electrifying sights
and sounds.

Remember the umbrella metaphor that we introduced in chapter 1? God's plan has always been to dwell among his people and to make his presence known. Even after banishing Adam and Eve from the garden of Eden, God pursued his plan to provide a dwelling place for his people. The Sinai experience was another step in that overarching design.

Of course, the Israelites couldn't stay indefinitely at the base of that mountain. With the future in mind, God provided them with some principles for worship and also communicated detailed instructions for building a mobile tent to be used for worship as his people traveled to the promised land. God understood the importance of giving his covenant people a place to house the holiness of the Mount Sinai experience of divine presence as they journeyed onward. From Exodus 19–40, we find the Israelites still camped out at the location of Mount Sinai.

Fig. 4.1. Umbrella: God's Plan to Dwell with Us

God Reveals Principles for Entering His Presence

Eventually, God's people would move on through the barren wilderness of the Sinai Peninsula on their journey to the promised land of milk and honey. How would they worship God while they were in transit? God answered with timeless principles in the first table of the Ten Commandments.

Did you ever stop to realize what percentage of the commandments focus on worship? Forty percent—the first four. We can summarize this part of the Decalogue as follows:

Commandment	Focus	Meaning for Worship
First: "You shall have no other gods before me" (Ex. 20:3)	Object of true worship	Worship must be given to the true God exclusively. Don't worship the wrong God.
Second: "You shall not make for yourself an image in the form of anything in heaven above or on the earth beneath or in the waters below. You shall not bow down to them or worship them" (Ex. 20:4–5)	Manner of worship	Worship should focus on the spiritual rather than on physical, visible images. Don't worship the true God in the wrong way.
Third: "You shall not misuse the name of the LORD your God" (Ex. 20:7)	Attitude for worship	Worship requires a reverent heart attitude.
Fourth: "Remember the Sabbath day by keeping it holy" (Ex. 20:8)	Time of worship	Worship requires one day out of seven to be set aside for its purpose.

God's people not only needed to get off on the right foot by knowing *how* to worship[1] but also needed to know *where* to worship. We will soon see that God provided them with instructions for this.

Locations for Worship

One of the highlights of my travels over the past few decades has been the privilege of participating in worship services in a variety of different cultures—sometimes as a guest preacher, other times by slipping unnoticed into a seat to worship along with fellow believers who may or may not speak my language. Stored in my memory forever is the experience of speaking in a tin-roofed, open-air sanctuary in Uganda to a congregation of African Christians who pretended to understand every word I spoke. To this day, their loud, joyful singing reverberates in my heart! Another cherished memory is that of preaching in a darkened but packed church in a rural village in Romania in borrowed clothes (my luggage hadn't made the trip to my destination airport!). This was my first experience of preaching to a segregated congregation—the men sat on one side and the women on the other.

If you have had the privilege of worshipping with believers in other parts of the world, or even in different churches just within your own country, you know there is great variety across sacred spaces. Simple or elaborate, small or massive, indoors or outdoors, urban or rural, formal or casual . . . the list could go on. But it wasn't always this way in the "sacred spaces" where God's people worshipped.

Scripture tells us that the first sacred (or holy) space was a garden—the garden of Eden. During the lives of the patriarchs

---

1. Helpful explanations of the first four commandments can be found in the Westminster Shorter Catechism, questions 45–62, the Westminster Larger Catechism, questions 102–21, and the Heidelberg Catechism, questions 94–103.

(Abraham, Isaac, and Jacob), God's people erected new sacred spaces for worship in the form of altars, and families gathered around these altars to call on the name of the Lord. Generations later, God's people again gathered—this time at the foot of Mount Sinai. Their numbers had grown to hundreds of thousands by this time. As this massive population prepared for a major trek toward the promised land, the people may well have wondered where they would worship once they left the mountain.

God made his intentions clear: "Have them make a sacred tent for me. I will live among them" (Ex. 25:8 NIrV). And what was this to be like? God gave them careful and detailed instructions for building a sacred portable tent by employing artistic details and costly materials. This included

> gold, silver and bronze; blue, purple and scarlet yarn and fine linen; goat hair; ram skins dyed red and another type of durable leather; acacia wood; olive oil for the light; spices for the anointing oil and for the fragrant incense; and onyx stones and other gems to be mounted on the ephod and breastpiece. (Ex. 25:3–7)

Notice the inclusion of metals, dyed yarns, fabrics, timber, oil, spices, and gems in beautiful harmony. Why such attention to detail? The New Testament makes clear that this tabernacle was designed to be an earthly copy and shadow of the heavenly sanctuary (see Heb. 8:5). Worship would be otherworldly in the sense that it would provide entry into a world that reflected the reality of the heavenly dimension.

Per God's instructions, the tabernacle was to be placed inside an outer courtyard, which was equivalent in length to half of an American football field. Within the courtyard was a bronze laver for washing and a bronze altar for sacrificing. The tent structure itself was divided by a hanging curtain into two chambers: the Holy Place, which was fifteen by thirty feet, and the inner Most Holy

Place, which was fifteen by fifteen feet. Inside the Holy Place was a golden table for the bread of the presence, a golden lampstand (which was symbolic of the tree of life in the garden of Eden), and an incense altar. The central article of furniture in the Most Holy Place was the ark of the covenant—a gold-covered chest with a "mercy seat" lid. Two golden cherubim with outstretched wings sat atop the chest, perhaps looking over the mystery of atonement.[2]

Significance of the Tabernacle

Truth be told, it's all too easy to become overwhelmed when you attempt to understand and retain all the details of the tabernacle and its furnishings while at the same time sorting out their significance as they point to Christ. It's easy to get bogged down in subjective allegorical interpretations of the tabernacle, which we can see happening all the way back in the time of Philo of Alexandria (20 BC–AD 50), who claimed to see in the tabernacle the universe in miniature. No need to refute that! So let's forgo a detailed inventory of the tabernacle and its furnishings and instead look at the bigger picture as it relates to our worship today.

Exactly what was the theological significance of the tabernacle? This transportable tent demonstrated spiritual truth in a visible manner by acting as a necessary "wrapping" for the invisible God when he came down to be present with his people. The narratives in the book of Exodus that tell the story of the construction of the tabernacle have been called "visual aids of spiritual realities."[3] Let's take a look at some of the spiritual truths that were revealed in the tabernacle that pointed ahead to Christ.

---

2. Perhaps this relates to Peter's comment that "even angels long to look into these things" (1 Peter 1:12).

3. J. A. Motyer, *The Message of Exodus: The Days of Our Pilgrimage* (Downers Grove, IL: IVP Academic, 2005), 250.

Separation

In a tangible way, the tabernacle demonstrated the separation that exists between God and humans in a post-fall world. This separation was visibly portrayed by a veil (a finely woven curtain embroidered with figures of angels) that divided the Holy Place from the Most Holy Place. Only the high priest could enter the Most Holy Place, and only once a year. Both the veil and the priests' mediation served to protect the people from the holy wrath of God now that the immediacy of garden worship was no longer possible.

Presence

The tabernacle was a visible reminder to the people that God had chosen to reveal his presence to his worshippers. He carefully instructed Moses to "have them make a sanctuary for me, and I will dwell among them" and promised, "I will meet with you" (Ex. 25:8, 22).

Can we be sure that God kept that promise? Four indications of divine presence in the tabernacle assure us that he did.

The names of the tabernacle. Scripture uses names for the tabernacle that indicate God's presence. For example, it is called a "dwelling place" (*Mishkan*), because its location—wherever that might be—was the place where God chose to fulfill his covenant promise to dwell with his people. The God of the garden of Eden, who also made himself known to the patriarchs at the sites of various altars, now moved with his people and chose to dwell with them.

If you are a student of American history, you may know that many colonial New Englanders called their churches "meeting houses." This name harked back to another name for the tabernacle: the Tent of Meeting (*Ohel-Moed*). As the people assembled at the tent for worship, the Lord indeed chose to meet with them.

The tabernacle was also designated as the Holy Place (*Mikdash*), because it was set apart by God's holy presence in its precincts.

Whenever any of these names were employed for the tabernacle, they reinforced the truth that the Lord would be there.

Names for the Tabernacle	
Dwelling Place	Mishkan
Tent of Meeting	Ohel-Moed
Holy Place	Mikdash

The ark of the covenant. True, this golden chest was hidden behind the curtain in the darkened Most Holy Place, which only the High Priest was able to enter once a year. Nevertheless, the people knew that the ark of the covenant was there.

The top lid of the ark was called the mercy seat, or atonement cover. Second Samuel 6:2 refers to the Lord being enthroned at the ark. The implication is that the ark served as a kind of visible throne for the invisible King of Kings on earth. The ark is also referred to as the footstool of God (see 1 Chron. 28:2; Ps. 99:5; 132:7).

Overshadowing the ark were two golden cherubim—winged guardians that designated this sacred space as the abode of God. Scripture speaks of "the LORD, who is enthroned between the cherubim" (1 Chron. 13:6). Recall that cherubim had stood guard at the entrance of the garden of Eden. Now they guarded the Lord's presence by overshadowing the ark.

Archaeologists have discovered that it was not uncommon for arks that were found in ancient pagan temples to contain images of a deity. But the tabernacle differs, as did the later temple, in that it contained no images of God whatsoever. This was in keeping with God's prohibition of images in the second commandment.

What Happened to the Ark?

George Lucas and Steven Spielberg had fun using their brilliant imaginations to produce the blockbuster action film *Indiana Jones and the Raiders of the Lost Ark*. In the film, archaeologist Dr. Indiana Jones jets around the world in a frantic effort to keep the ark of the covenant out of the hands of the Nazis. This adventure takes him to Nepal, Cairo, and an island in the Aegean Sea. Ranked as one of the five hundred greatest movies of all time, this fictional film illustrates people's ongoing fascination with the ark. Just as in the movie, the final location of the biblical ark of the covenant remains a mystery.

The table of the bread of presence. To the right, as one entered the tabernacle, was a small table on which rested "the bread of the Presence" (Ex. 25:30) and utensils for eating, which conveyed the Lord's invitation to a meal. The fact that God was present can be seen in the words "before me" from that verse, which are translated from the Hebrew *panim* (which can also be translated "face"). This term is used elsewhere in Scripture to represent the presence of God.[4]

The priests in the Old Testament would have understood that when they came to the table, they came before the face of God.

> This bread is to be set out before the LORD regularly, Sabbath after Sabbath, on behalf of the Israelites, as a lasting covenant. It belongs to Aaron and his sons, who are to eat it in the

---

4. See, for example, Psalm 27:8: "My heart says of you, 'Seek his *face!*' Your *face*, LORD, I will seek." Also note the Aaronic benediction that is often used at the conclusion of worship services: "The LORD bless you and keep you; the LORD make his *face* shine on you and be gracious to you; the LORD turn his *face* toward you and give you peace" (Num. 6:24–26). *Face* is used as an anthropomorphism. Worship is seeking the face of God.

sanctuary area, because it is a most holy part of their perpetual share of the food offerings presented to the LORD. (Lev. 24:8–9)

Some see, in this Old Testament "type," a foreshadowing of our repeated coming to the Lord's table as we partake of bread in his presence.

The glory cloud (Kabod). The cloud that filled the tabernacle at its dedication and accompanied the Israelites through their time of wilderness wanderings was another symbolic reminder of God's presence. Read what occurred at the dedication.

Then the cloud covered the tent of meeting, and the glory of the LORD filled the tabernacle. Moses could not enter the tent of meeting because the cloud had settled on it, and the glory of the LORD filled the tabernacle. (Ex. 40:34–35)

Once again the heavy sense of God's presence that had been experienced at Mount Sinai fell on Moses. He was so overwhelmed by God's transcendent glory that he was unable to enter the tabernacle. There was no mistaking it—God had come. And the glory cloud that represented his presence remained with his people on their journey.

In all the travels of the Israelites, whenever the cloud lifted from above the tabernacle, they would set out. . . . So the cloud of the LORD was over the tabernacle by day, and fire was in the cloud by night, in the sight of all the Israelites during all their travels. (Ex. 40:36, 38)

A. W. Tozer may have had this event in mind when he reminded us that "worship is not some performance we do, but a Presence we experience."[5] Tozer also raised this provocative point: "If God was still giving the same signals of His abiding Presence, I wonder how many churches would have the approving cloud by day and fire by night."[6]

Centrality

The conspicuous centrality of worship to the people's daily life was demonstrated by the placement of the tabernacle. Per God's instructions, the tabernacle was positioned in the very center of the camp. God then assigned the twelve tribes to specific locations surrounding the tabernacle: "The Israelites are to camp around the tent of meeting some distance from it, each of them under their standard and holding the banners of their family" (Num. 2:2).

This arrangement would not have surprised the Israelites, given that Ancient Near Eastern monarchs typically placed their tents in the center of an encampment to be surrounded by their people. In preparation for battle, both the Assyrian and Babylonian armies followed this layout and positioned their tents to surround the king's tent. But the King of Kings had strategically placed his tent in the center of the camp of his people for the purpose of worship, not battle.

This concept is reflected in the layout of medieval European cities, in which tall cathedral spires are often the first thing that you notice as you approach. The town square almost always has a structure devoted to worship. The same layout can be seen in many early New England towns. While I was living in Connecticut, I never tired of visiting old historic towns within driving distance of my home. Can you guess what many of them had in common?

---

5. A. W. Tozer, *The Purpose of Man: Designed to Worship*, comp. and ed. James L. Snyder (repr., Minneapolis: Bethany House, 2009), 177.

6. Kevin P. Emmert, ed., *Worship: The Reason We Were Created—Collected Insights from A. W. Tozer* (Chicago: Moody, 2017), 26.

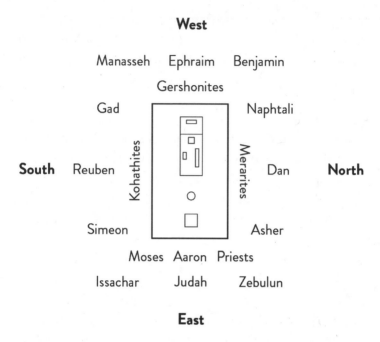

Fig. 4.2. Placement of the Tribes around the Tabernacle

It was a centrally located town green, around which had been built at least one (but often several) tall, white-steepled churches. Many of the churches had been constructed in the 1600s and 1700s. The presence of such a church on the town green made the visual statement that worship was central to the life of that community.

What about your community? What's the central focal point of life in your town—the mall, the convention center, the corporate headquarters, the sports arena? How often is it a place of worship?

What Did Worship Look Like at the Tabernacle?

Most of us know what to expect when we attend a service of worship—at least in the tradition and tribe in which we were raised or to which we have become accustomed. Many commonalities cross denominational and even geographical lines. I would venture to guess, however, that few people are familiar with what took place inside the tabernacle when the Israelites assembled for worship.

Scripture tells us that the heart of tabernacle worship was the sacrificial system of the ceremonial law, which was appropriate for that particular time in the history of redemption. That system was instituted with the covenant offerings Moses made at Mount Sinai to atone for the sins of the people (see Ex. 24:4–8). The blood sacrifices were offered to objectively provide atonement for sin and to propitiate God's holy wrath. These sacrifices prefigured the one perfect atonement that would be made by Christ on the cross. Thus, God's instructions concerning the sacrifices to be made on the altars at the tabernacle were detailed and specific.

The Israelite people were not allowed inside the tabernacle; they were permitted to stand only outside in the courtyard. The sacrifices were to be mediated by priests from the caste that was formed from Aaron and his descendants. It was their responsibility to represent the people before God in the offering of sacrifices—to "do the *work* at the LORD's tabernacle" (Num. 16:9). The word in the Septuagint Greek translation of the Hebrew Old Testament that is translated into English here as "work" is *leitourgia*. It is a source of the English word *liturgy*. At this time in Israel's history, liturgy was not the work of the people but rather the work of the priests in the Old Testament tabernacle.

Praise God that things are different now. Moses related God's intention at Mount Sinai that "you will be for me a kingdom of priests and a holy nation" (Ex. 19:6). When the incarnate Son of God came to earth, he assumed the role of our Great High Priest. All those who are united to Christ are now priests; they have direct access to God and are able to participate actively in the "liturgy"—that is, the activities that occur in a worship service.

What does this mean for you and me? First Peter 2:5 indicates that we "are being built into a spiritual house to be a holy priesthood, offering spiritual sacrifices acceptable to God through Jesus Christ." The good news is that sacrificial worship is no longer the privilege of a special priestly class. As the Protestant Reformers stressed, we now enjoy the priesthood of all believers. Revelation 1:6 similarly reminds us that Jesus "has made us to be a kingdom and priests to serve his God and Father." This means that each time you and I gather for worship, we are in fact exercising our priestly responsibilities and privileges as we participate in singing, enter into prayer, offer up tithes and offerings, and partake of the Lord's Supper. How different things are for us than they were for God's people, who were left standing outside in the courtyard of the tabernacle.

A Misplaced Sense of Longing for the Past

But could we be missing something? Some might conjecture, with a tinge of longing, that the sense of God's presence must have been overwhelming for the people of Israel in a way that can never be duplicated today. The colors, the tapestries, the visible cloud and pillar of fire are no longer a part of our worship experience.

But Scripture teaches us clearly that tabernacle worship was inferior to what we have today. Simply put, tabernacle worship in the Old Testament was an incomplete type and shadow that pointed ahead to Christ. It served its purpose and was used for only three hundred to four hundred years before it was replaced. Once God's people entered the promised land, they carried the tabernacle and ark of the covenant over a period of years to Gilgal, to Shechem, to Ebal, and then to Shiloh. The ark was next moved to Gibean, but it's not clear whether the tabernacle was still in existence to make that move along with the Ark. The tabernacle era came to an end, as the people waited for the fulfillment that Christ would bring.

74

Tabernacle Nostalgia

Appreciation for the tabernacle, and perhaps a bit of nostalgia, have contributed to the naming of buildings and even towns. One example that comes to mind is a church that was erected in southern New Jersey in 1778 by the missionary brothers John and David Brainerd. The church was named the Tabernacle in the Wilderness. To this day, the town is called Tabernacle Township. The original church building was eventually converted into a one-room schoolhouse, and later the Tabernacle Methodist Episcopal Church was built on the same site. Anyone who is in search of an authentic tabernacle worship experience will need to look elsewhere.

Fulfillment Means That We Have It Better

A verse that we often hear at Christmastime is wonderful news at any time of the year. John 1:14 says, "The Word [Christ] became flesh and made his dwelling among us." The verb that is translated into English as "made his dwelling" is *skenow*. It is used in the Septuagint as the noun form of the word for "tabernacle." You and I no longer need to erect a tabernacle for our worship assemblies, because Christ himself has come to tabernacle among us. The Word became flesh and tented among us. To say it another way, Christ brought fulfillment to the tabernacle through his incarnation.

Christ similarly fulfilled the tabernacle by revealing his glory. In that same verse we read, "We have seen his glory, the glory of the one and only Son, who came from the Father." The English word "glory" here comes from the Greek term *doxa*, which is the equivalent of the Hebrew word *Kabed*, which means "to be heavy or weighty." At the tabernacle, the weighty glory cloud filled the tent and hovered over it. That glory cloud denoted the awesome presence of God.

Do we ever see that cloud again? Yes, we do. The apostle John testified that he had seen God's glory. In chapter 9 we will see in greater detail what happened at the Mount of Transfiguration: "Peter and his companions were very sleepy, but when they became fully awake, they saw his glory. . . . A cloud appeared and covered them" (Luke 9:32, 34). The God who had manifested himself in the tabernacle had now come in physical form to planet Earth.

Christ also fulfilled the requirements of the sacrificial laws regarding animal sacrifices. He was the perfect Lamb of God; he serves as our Great High Priest. He is the reason we no longer need to offer altar sacrifices in order to find acceptance in God's holy presence. No longer are we left standing outside in the courtyard. No longer does a heavy curtain separate the Most Holy Place of God's presence. From Hebrews 9:11–12, we learn that "when Christ came as high priest of the good things that are now already here, he went through the greater and more perfect tabernacle that is not made with human hands, that is to say, is not a part of this creation. He did not enter by means of the blood of goats and calves; but he entered the Most Holy Place once for all by his own blood, thus obtaining eternal redemption."

The tabernacle was never designed to be permanent—only temporary. Later in the history of God's people, it was replaced by a more permanent temple. That's what we will look at in our next chapter.

Questions for Reflection and Discussion

1. Describe the relationship between the Ten Commandments and worship.
2. What were the sacred places for worship from the time of creation until the construction of the tabernacle?
3. How can you explain the theological significance of the tabernacle?

4. Summarize the significance of the location of the tabernacle in the camp. This chapter raised a question about the central focal point of life in your town. How would you describe what the typical residents of your community think about the implications of Christian worship?

5. What are some ways that our churches today can encourage the priesthood of believers in our worship services?

6. How does the tabernacle point to Christ?

7. Look again at the two quotations by A. W. Tozer in this chapter. Do you agree or disagree with them? Tozer died in 1963. If he were to come back and visit our churches today, do you think he might say the same thing, or might his assessment change?

5

A DARKENED ROOM FULL
OF VALUABLE TREASURES

Mount Zion: Mountain
of Temple Worship

Entering the house of God to dwell with God, beholding,
glorifying, and enjoying him eternally, I suggest, is the story of
the Bible, the plot that makes sense of the various acts, persons
and places of its pages, the deepest context for its doctrines.
—L. Michael Morales, *Who Shall Ascend*
the Mountain of the Lord?

"A mile wide but an inch deep." I've often heard this cliché invoked to describe the state of Christianity in Africa. Yet in my travels I have been encouraged to observe a new generation of African students and leaders who are strongly motivated to dig deeper into Scripture and reach their peers with the gospel, despite the relative paucity of biblical print and digital resources in that continent. North American Christians, however, have long enjoyed an abundance of Bibles, books, and biblical resources. Yet increasingly they demonstrate an appalling lack of even the most basic understanding of Scripture. After conducting a survey to measure Americans' knowledge of the Bible, Christian pollster George Barna concluded, "Americans revere the Bible—but, by and large, they don't read it. And because they don't read it, they have become a nation of biblical illiterates."[1]

A national survey of American millennials, who were then in their teens, revealed that many of them have settled for a kind of moralistic therapeutic deism. What kind of God do they worship? "This God is not trinitarian, he did not speak through the Torah or the prophets of Israel, was never resurrected from the dead, and does not fill and transform people through his Spirit. This God is not demanding. He actually can't be, because his job is to solve our problems and make people feel good. In short, God is something like a combination Divine Butler and Cosmic Therapist: he is always on call, takes care of any problems that arise, professionally helps his people to feel better about themselves, and does not become too personally involved in the process."[2]

Certainly we expect biblical illiteracy outside the church and should see it as a motivation for evangelism. But we should be especially concerned about biblical illiteracy within the church, because our understanding of Scripture informs our worship. Our view of God directly shapes our worship practices and our worship experiences. In this chapter, we will examine some frequently overlooked passages from the Old Testament. These passages describe events on another mountain and should shape our experience of worship and our view of God.

1. George Gallup Jr. and Jim Castelli, *The People's Religion: American Faith in the 90's* (New York: Macmillan, 1989), 60, quoted in R. Albert Mohler Jr., "The Scandal of Biblical Illiteracy: It's Our Problem," AlbertMohler.com, The Southern Baptist Theological Seminary, January 20, 2016, https://albertmohler.com/2016/01/20/the-scandal-of-biblical-illiteracy-its-our-problem-4/.

2. Christian Smith with Melinda Lundquist Denton, *Soul Searching: The Religious and Spiritual Lives of American Teenagers* (2005; repr., New York: Oxford University Press, 2009), 165.

The Old Testament can be likened to a darkened room that is full of valuable treasures waiting to be discovered. Let's turn on the lights in order to examine some of these treasures and see their implications for our worship.

Circumstances That Led to the Building of a Temple

The story begins with the yearning of a famous Middle Eastern king named David. Near the end of his life, he called together an assembly in Jerusalem. Among those whom he invited were officers, commanders, property officials, palace officials, and military personnel, including his brave fighting men. David stood before this assembly of national leaders and spoke these words: "Listen to me, my fellow Israelites, my people. I had it in my heart to build a house as a place of rest for the ark of the covenant of the LORD, for the footstool of our God, and I made plans to build it. But God said to me, 'You are not to build a house for my Name, because you are a warrior and have shed blood'" (1 Chron. 28:2–3).

David went on to explain to the crowd, "Of all my sons—and the LORD has given me many—he has chosen my son Solomon to sit on the throne of the kingdom of the LORD over Israel. He said to me: 'Solomon your son is the one who will build my house and my courts'" (1 Chron. 28:5). Then David turned over the detailed plans for the temple to his son, indicating that the Lord's hand would be on him. He left this challenge with Solomon: "Be strong and courageous, and do the work. Do not be afraid or discouraged, for the LORD God, my God, is with you. He will not fail you or forsake you until all the work for the service of the temple of the LORD is finished" (1 Chron. 28:20).

Against this backdrop, Solomon ascended the throne. He soon began preparation for the construction of the temple that his father, David, had turned over to him, according to God's direction. It was not until the fourth year of his reign—on the second day of the second month of Ziv (April or May)—that Solomon actually commenced construction of the temple of worship. Four hundred and eighty years had passed since the exodus from Egypt. At last the long-standing dream of a permanent place of worship was about to become a reality. I suspect that Solomon could not have imagined the lasting historical impact that this building would have. "No other building of the ancient world, either while it stood in Jerusalem or in the millennia since its final destruction, has been the focus of so much attention throughout the ages."[3]

Location of Construction

Where did this construction project take place, and why that location? The text pinpoints the spot as Mount Moriah, which is sometimes called Mount Zion, in Jerusalem (see 2 Chron. 3:1). Several geographical factors may have shaped this choice.

Central Location

The city of Jerusalem was located on the land bridge between the three main continents of Africa, Asia, and Europe. Crowds of travelers navigated through this city as they moved from one continent to another. Jerusalem was also strategically located near several intersecting highways, including the Ridge Road—a major north-south trade route in Israel. In 1581, the German pastor and cartographer Heinrich Bunting created a book of woodcut maps, the most famous of which was a map of three leaves that were joined together with a circle in the center. The three leaves of

---

3. C. M. Meyers, s.v. "Temple, Jerusalem," in *The Anchor Bible Dictionary*, ed. David Noel Freedman, vol. 6, *Si–Z* (New York: Doubleday, 1992), 350.

this clover represented Africa, Europe, and Asia, while the city of Jerusalem rested clearly in the center circle. In Ezekiel 5:5, God describes the city this way: "Jerusalem, which I have set in the center of the nations, with countries all around her."

Fig. 5.1. Bunting's Clover Leaf Map

Defensible Site

In addition, the city of Jerusalem was built on a site that could be defended against enemy attack. Within the city, walls encircled the elevated temple site on Mount Moriah. Narrow, deeply cut valleys surrounded the city on three sides and led up to mountain ridges. Only to the north was the city vulnerable to enemy attack. On several occasions, my wife and I have had the opportunity of visiting the Mount of Olives, which overlooks the Temple Mount and the city of Jerusalem to the west. Each time, we have recalled the words of the psalmist with new appreciation: "As the mountains surround Jerusalem, so the LORD surrounds his people" (Ps. 125:2).

What Is the Dome of the Rock?

During the days of Solomon's reign, about five thousand people lived in this holy city, which covered about thirty-two acres. Today, if you visit Jerusalem, you'll find a thriving metropolis that occupies about one hundred times more space and has a population of over eight hundred thousand. Inside the walls of the Old City, you can easily locate the Temple Mount, but the temple itself is gone. Instead you will see an iconic landmark— the golden-domed, octagonal Dome of the Rock shrine, which was completed in AD 691 and has exterior tiles featuring geometric designs and lengthy quotations from the Qur'an.

Muslims believe, as referenced in surah 17:6 of the Qur'an, that this shrine marks the spot where Muhammad ascended on his night journey to heaven. An indentation in the rock inside the building is believed by some to be the footprint of the prophet's steed as he pushed off in his ascent to heaven. Others believe that the impression in the rock is the footprint of Muhammad himself. Yet others explain it as the imprint that was left by God's own foot when he completed the creation of the world at this site. The fourth-century Christian pilgrim Egeria believed that the indentation in the rock was the footprint of the infant Jesus, which was created on the occasion when he was presented in the temple to the Lord and blessed by Simeon. Lots of wild speculation—all of it unproven.

Contrary to popular misunderstanding, the Dome of the Rock is not a mosque but rather a Muslim shrine that was built over the rock that is traditionally thought to be the site where Abraham prepared to sacrifice his son Isaac before God intervened. This Islamic shrine is the third most sacred site for Muslims. Due to the threat of terrorism in recent years,

---

tourists must contend with the highest levels of security when attempting to visit this shrine. Bibles and other religious materials are strongly forbidden at the site. Passports are required, and visitors are screened with metal detectors. It wasn't always this way. In past years, visitors—myself included—found it much easier to gain entrance into the Temple Mount and the Dome of the Rock. The only restriction was that visitors would be asked to leave their shoes outside the entrance. Tourists who wish to visit the Temple Mount today should not expect to gain such easy access to this holy site. Much patience and persistence will be required. On a recent visit to Jerusalem, I attempted on three separate occasions to enter the shrine but encountered extremely limited visiting hours and rebuffs from patrolling Islamic guards. This came as no surprise. The Temple Mount is, after all, considered by some to be the most contested piece of real estate on earth. It's revered by Muslims, Christians, and Jews alike.

Sacred and Historical Significance

Throughout Old Testament history, Mount Moriah was a sacred place for offering sacrifices to God.[4] Not only is it likely the mountain in Jerusalem where Abraham willingly prepared to offer his son Isaac, but it was also the place where David faced a life-changing encounter—first with Satan and then with the angel of the Lord.

Israel had achieved a string of military victories against its enemies when the archenemy, Satan, rose up and incited King David to call for a census to be taken of all the people in the land. You may be thinking, "What's wrong with taking a census?"

---

4. Some commentators suggest that near where Abraham was willing to offer up his son Isaac, God the Father willingly offered up his Son as a redemptive sacrifice.

Usually nothing—but in this case, David commanded the census without waiting for the Lord's permission. His decision may have been motivated by pride—by wanting to know the size of his empire or the number of his military forces. Large numbers would entitle him to bragging rights and would be a tribute to his own strength and power.

Joab, the commander of David's troops, wisely counseled the king that moving ahead with this census would bring guilt on Israel because God had not commanded it. Whatever David's rationale for the census was, it was to his peril that he disregarded the counsel of his commander. When the census was completed, David learned that there were 1,100,000 men in Israel plus almost a half million more in Judah.

In the end, however, David's disobedience proved to be costly. As punishment for it, the Lord sent a plague on Israel that killed seventy thousand men. But at the last minute, he mercifully withdrew his hand from destroying the entire population of Jerusalem.

This incident is recorded in 1 Chronicles 21. "David looked up and saw the angel of the LORD standing between heaven and earth, with a drawn sword in his hand extended over Jerusalem. Then David and the elders clothed in sackcloth, fell facedown" (v. 16). A repentant David admitted the depth of his sin and was told by his seer that God wanted him to build an altar to the Lord on the threshing floor that belonged to Araunah the Jebusite. When David approached Araunah with the request to purchase the land, the landowner agreed.

In obedience to God, David erected an altar and offered sacrifices to him on that location. His prayer for mercy and his sacrificial offering were answered dramatically with fire from heaven. There could be no doubt that this was a sacred spot. Fittingly, it would become the future site for the building of the temple.

God's Move into the Temple

After David died, in the fourth year of his son Solomon's reign, plans for the building of the temple commenced. The actual construction took place over a period of seven long years and was completed in 959 BC during the Feast of Tabernacles, in the seventh month of the year—equivalent to our September or October. Let's take a closer look at several events from 2 Chronicles 5:2–6:11 and 7:1–2 that occurred that autumn in connection with the people's completion and God's occupying of what some have called the most important building in history.

Moving the Ark In

Once the sacred building was completed, furnishings needed to be added to it. Conspicuously absent from these furnishings was any image of God. "Throughout the Near East, temples included an anthropomorphic representation—a cult statue—of the deity who 'lived' in the temple. But there was no such image or statue in the Israelite temple. This is a major distinction between the Israelite's Temple and all other Near Eastern temples."[5] Instead of an image, the ark of the covenant was moved into the new temple's Holy of Holies.

You'll recall that in the original portable tabernacle, the ark of the covenant could be carried from one place to another—it was a mobile shrine. This gold-covered chest with its cherubim had rested in the Holy of Holies, or Most Holy Place, of the tabernacle until the Israelites arrived in the promised land. In the years that followed, the ark was moved from place to place. Eventually it was located in the city of David—an outlying cone-shaped spur of land that was south of the Temple Mount, just outside the city

---

5. Hershel Shanks, *Jerusalem's Temple Mount: From Solomon to the Golden Dome* (New York: Continuum International, 2007), 139.

walls of Jerusalem. Today it is an archaeological park that contains the most extensive section of Old Testament Jerusalem sites that can be visited. Under Solomon, the Levites relocated the ark a short distance to its new home in the new temple. Inside the chest-like ark were the tables of the Ten Commandments that were originally given to Moses on another mountain. These physical tables were a reminder to the people of the link between Mount Sinai and Mount Zion.

Can you begin to picture this? A glorious temple had been completed. But don't imagine a large building; Solomon's temple wasn't as large as most churches in North America today. Inside that small building was an even smaller inner chamber—a windowless dark room—in which the Levites placed the ark. The darkness of that room represented the reality that the invisible God of the universe cannot be seen with our physical eyes.

For generations, the people of Israel had looked to the ark as the focus of God's visitation on earth. Its presence reminded them that even though God dwells in heaven, he is always available to his people when they pray. It is not surprising that on this occasion, Solomon came to the temple and broke forth into a glorious prayer of worship that flows through most of the forty-two verses of 2 Chronicles 6. Toward the conclusion of his prayer, he said, "Now arise, LORD God, and come to your resting place, you and the ark of your might" (v. 41). And God did! After generations, the ark of the covenant now safely rested in its new temple home, signifying that this home was now the dwelling place of God.

Dedication of the Temple

No celebration is complete without music. On this occasion, glorious worship music filled the air.

The priests then withdrew from the Holy Place. All the priests who were there had consecrated themselves, regardless of their divisions. All the Levites who were musicians—Asaph, Heman, Jeduthun and their sons and relatives—stood on the east side of the altar, dressed in fine linen and playing cymbals, harps and lyres. They were accompanied by 120 priests sounding trumpets. The trumpeters and musicians joined in unison to give praise and thanks to the LORD. Accompanied by trumpets, cymbals and other instruments, the singers raised their voices in praise to the LORD and sang:

> "He is good;
> his love endures forever." (2 Chron. 5:11–13)

Wouldn't you have loved to have been there just to hear the music? Early Near Eastern texts as well as paintings at archaeological sites reveal that a wide range of musical instruments were in use at that time in history. The variety of instruments employed on this occasion was a fitting accompaniment to the rich lyrics that were sung to celebrate the attributes of God. Both the words in this text as well as the lyrics that are used throughout the Psalms should reinforce the importance of God-centered music in our worship services. How does your church measure up? Is there room for improvement?

Coming of the Cloud

The ark has been moved into its new home, the musicians respond with glorious music, and then it happens—another theophany.

> Then the temple of the LORD was filled with the cloud, and the priests could not perform their service because of the cloud, for the glory of the LORD filled the temple of God.
> Then Solomon said, "The LORD has said that he would dwell in a dark cloud; I have built a magnificent temple for you, a place for you to dwell forever." (2 Chron. 5:13–6:2)

The Hebrew word that is translated "glory" is *kabod*. In this context it is used to describe God's presence at the temple on Mount Zion—weighty, heavy, awesome.[6] You'll recall that on Mount Sinai the cloud had first descended to reveal the glory of God's presence at the summit assembly. Again at the tabernacle dedication, the glory of God filled the tent. Even after the tabernacle was no longer used, the glory of God also accompanied the ark of the covenant. Now as the new temple is dedicated, the transcendent glory of God, represented by a cloud, again fills the sacred place of worship.

Glory Cloud

Mt. Sinai   **Tabernacle**   **Temple**

Fig. 5.2. Recurrence of the Glory Cloud

Why a cloud? Perhaps God chose this form because it was something visible that conveyed a sense of mystery. A heavy, dark cloud would also serve as a shield to protect human eyes from looking directly at God's glory. Priests who served in the temple would especially need protection from a lethal dose of God's glory—it would be too overwhelming for them to stand directly in God's presence. The atmosphere at the temple dedication was heavy with the actual visitation of the transcendent God.

It seems that God first revealed his glory exclusively to the

6. *Kabod* is also used in non-theological contexts to describe Eli's weight (see 1 Sam. 4:18), Absalom's hair (see 2 Sam. 14:26), Moses's mouth and tongue (see Ex. 4:10), and Abraham's wealth (see Gen. 13:2).

priests. His presence within the temple was so overpowering that the priests were completely unable to perform their priestly duties. Later in the dedication, his glory would be seen by all.

Fire from Heaven

As part of the dedication ceremony, 22,000 head of cattle and 120,000 sheep and goats were sacrificed. The size of the offering no doubt reflected the intensity of Solomon's devotion to God and the unique significance of this dedication event. But the size of the offering wasn't the most significant thing. Second Chronicles 7:1 tells us, "When Solomon finished praying, fire came down from heaven and consumed the burnt offering and the sacrifices." Imagine what it must have been like to witness this. Fire has a way of attracting attention; as a symbol of power, it can't be ignored.

This was not the first time that God had sent fire from heaven. Nor would it be the last. We already saw that God answered David's sacrifice at Araunah's threshing floor with fire from heaven. We also saw that when God's people assembled with Moses at Mount Sinai, fire emanating from the presence of God descended on the mountaintop and consumed the burnt offering. All the people who were present shouted joyfully as they fell facedown in worship (see Lev. 9:24). And there were other occasions when this happened, too. When Gideon built an altar and offered a sacrifice to the Lord, the angel of the Lord appeared, holding a staff in his hand. With the tip of his staff, he touched the sacrifice. "Fire flared from the rock, consuming the meat and the bread" (Judg. 6:21). The prophet Elijah engaged in a spirited contest with the prophets of Baal on another mountain, Mount Carmel, which we will visit in the next chapter. When he did, "the fire of the Lord fell and burned up the sacrifice, the wood, the stones and the soil, and also licked up the water in the trench" (1 Kings 18:38).

It's not surprising that at the dedication of the temple, God again sent down flames of fire to consume the sacrifices that were offered. The evidence of God's transcendent presence was dramatic and overwhelming.

God's Glory Fills the Temple

Then came the capstone event: the glory of the Lord filled the temple. It appears that God was displaying his glory not to a select group of priests, as before, but to all the people who had assembled for the dedication.

The response of the people is not all that surprising. What else can you do when you enter the presence of the Lord God other than to fall down and worship? The Hebrew word *shahah* is the most frequently used term for worship in the Old Testament. It means to bow down or prostrate oneself. The entire crowd did just that. Together they knelt on the pavement and fell facedown on the ground. They sang of the Lord's goodness and enduring love. The people experienced the glory of God in a *shahah* moment.

Implications of the Temple for Us

What do these events on Mount Zion mean for us?

The temple clearly points us to our need for Jesus Christ. It was merely a type and shadow, as the tabernacle had been. The repeated temple sacrifices called for more—a once-for-all atoning sacrifice that only Christ could make on the cross on Golgotha. This need for Christ was evident not only in the original temple that was built by Solomon but also in the temples that replaced it in subsequent years. Earthly temples in themselves were always incomplete without Christ. Solomon's temple was destroyed when the armies of the Babylonian king Nebuchadnezzar descended on Jerusalem in 586 BC. After seventy years of Babylonian captivity,

Zerubbabel, a descendant of David and governor of Judah, built a new temple whose magnificence and grandeur could not compare with those of Solomon's temple. But, generations later, Herod the Great significantly expanded Zerubbabel's temple. A rabbinic sage reportedly said, "He who has not seen the Temple of Herod has never seen a beautiful building."[7] When viewed from a distance, it was said, its glistening limestone and golden facade looked like a snow-clad mountain. Josephus, the first-century Jewish historian, wrote that when the sun shone on the temple at sunrise, people had to avert their eyes lest they be blinded.[8]

The New Testament records the story of when a devout and righteous man named Simeon was standing in Herod's temple on Mount Zion on the very day that Mary and Joseph walked into the temple to have their baby boy consecrated to the Lord. What had probably been an ordinary day for Simeon turned into anything but. Scripture tells us that Simeon had eagerly longed for the coming of the Lord's Messiah and had been promised by God that he would not die until he had seen the Messiah. Simeon immediately recognized the infant boy. Taking the child lovingly into his arms, he burst into a song of worship and praise to God.

Years later, that same person whom Simeon had held in his arms would drive out the greedy money changers and even dare to hint at the future destruction of the temple itself. History records that his prophecy was fulfilled when the Roman armies under Titus swept down on Jerusalem in AD 70, destroying the temple along with the city. Josephus describes the destruction graphically: "The roar of the flames streaming far and wide mingled with the groans of the falling victims; and, owing to the height of the hill and the mass of the burning pile, one would have thought that

7. Babylonian Talmud, *Baba Bathra* 4a.

8. See Josephus, *The Jewish War*, trans. H. St. J. Thackeray, Loeb Classical Library (Cambridge, MA: Harvard University Press, 1976), bk. 5.5.6, line 223, cited in Shanks, *Jerusalem's Temple Mount*, 63.

Simeon's Song

Simeon's well-known canticle is called the *Nunc Dimittis*, meaning "Now you dismiss." This title is the Latin translation of the words that appear near the opening of the song, which is recorded in Luke 2:29–32.

> Sovereign Lord, as you have promised,
>> you may *now dismiss* your servant in peace.
> For my eyes have seen your salvation,
>> which you have prepared in the sight of all nations:
> a light for revelation to the Gentiles,
>> and the glory of your people Israel.

---

the whole city was ablaze."[9] All that remains of the temple today are the colossal limestone rocks that form a retaining wall known as the Western Wall or Wailing Wall. The stones in the exposed part of the wall fit together precisely without the use of mortar and each weigh between one and eight tons.

Jesus referred to his incarnate body as the temple of God on earth (see John 2:21). His coming to earth meant that there was no longer a need for God to manifest himself in a glory cloud within a physical temple. The Old Testament temple had served its purpose as a type and shadow that pointed ahead to the coming of Christ. The good news is that you and I and all believers now enjoy direct access to Jesus Christ himself. He is far greater than the temple and replaces Mount Zion as the center of fulfillment. Let's not lament the loss of the physical temple but rather rejoice in the gift of Someone far better: Jesus Christ, who is the focal point of our worship.

9. Josephus, *Jewish War*, bk. 6.5.1, lines 271–272, quoted in Shanks, *Jerusalem's Temple Mount*, 104.

Recently I learned about a megachurch in Brazil that has constructed a replica of Solomon's temple designed to accommodate ten thousand worshippers—perhaps in an attempt to duplicate the spiritual experiences that occurred in that ancient temple. The stones used for the building were imported from Israel—at no small cost, I would imagine. Probably no one who stumbled on the church's website was surprised to see it soliciting donations to fund the rebuilding of Solomon's temple. Does this sound like moving backward to you? It does to me. We don't need to revisit or rebuild Solomon's temple. We have come to Jesus Christ.

That Brazilian church should serve as a reminder to us that the divine presence cannot be manipulated by architectural design or even creative programming. God will always sovereignly take the initiative in choosing to manifest his presence as he wills.

Christ fulfills all the forms and ceremonies of Old Testament worship that were incomplete and that pointed ahead to him. You and I don't need to recapture the worship that occurred in the Old Testament temple. The nature of New Testament worship should be Christ-centered. Consider how our worship services point to Christ:

- New Testament hymns celebrate Christ's nature and work (Phil. 2:6–11; Col. 1:15–20; 1 Tim. 3:16)
- Prayers are now offered in Christ's name (John 15:16; Eph. 5:20; Heb. 13:15)
- Confessions of faith acknowledge Christ's lordship (Rom. 10:9; 1 Cor. 12:3; Phil. 2:11)
- Baptism is performed in the name of the crucified and resurrected Christ (Acts 2:38; 22:16; Rom. 6:2–6; Gal. 3:27–28; Col. 2:12)
- The Lord's Supper centers on the death and promised return of the resurrected Christ (1 Cor. 11:26–29)
- The Lord's Day being the time of worship reminds us of

Christ, who was resurrected on the first day of the week (Matt. 28:1; Acts 20:7; 1 Cor. 16:2; Rev. 1:10)

Another thing that the temple on Mount Zion points us to is the centrality of the divine presence in worship. Participation in authentic worship today requires that we come by faith into the invisible presence of the triune God. Although we should not expect to see a visible glory cloud hovering over our heads at worship assemblies, we are in fact entering the invisible presence of God when we come with praise on our lips and prayers on our tongues. Worship is all about experiencing the glory of God.

I enjoy visiting the Western Wall in the Old City of Jerusalem each time I travel to Israel. Jews consider it to be a sacred site because they believe that this wall is the closest they can get to the location of what was once the Most Holy Place. The wall itself is part of the retaining wall that was built by King Herod during his expansion of the temple. Jews were prohibited from accessing this area from 1948 until the Six-Day War in 1967, when paratroopers captured the Old City of Jerusalem. Today the wall is a place of prayer.

On a recent visit to Jerusalem, I noted a sign that was mounted near the entrance to the Western Wall. I couldn't resist taking a photo. The words on the sign were written in both Hebrew and English: "Dear Visitors, You are approaching the holy site of the Western Wall where the Divine Presence always rests. Please make sure you are appropriately and modestly dressed so as not to cause harm to this holy place or to the feelings of the worshippers." Can you imagine if a similar sign were posted at the entrance to your church? *Dear visitors, you are entering into the glorious presence of God. Bow down before his glory and worship!*

Pastor and author John Piper writes, "The term 'glory of God' in the Bible generally refers to the visible splendor or moral beauty of God's manifold perfections. . . . It is an attempt to put into words what cannot be contained in words—what God is like in his unveiled magnificence and excellence."[10] We would do well to remember that the aim of our worship is not simply an intellectual comprehension of facts but rather the passionate and joyful admiration of God himself. In fact, this is the aim of our entire existence—we were created for nothing less. The rhythm of worship is that God reveals his glory so that we in turn can respond and give him glory. "*God is most glorified in us when we are most satisfied in him.*' And we find satisfaction in what we worship, in what we treasure, and what we delight in. We glorify God most by enjoying him . . . '*the chief end of man is to glorify God by enjoying him forever.*'"[11] May that be the goal of the lives that you and I live before the face of the triune God.

Questions for Reflection and Discussion

1. Do you agree or disagree that biblical illiteracy is a problem in today's churches? What can be done to raise people's level of biblical literacy?
2. What's the significance of the place where Solomon chose to build the temple?
3. What do we learn about the ark of the covenant and its role in temple worship?
4. Is there anything you spot in the music that was used at the temple dedication that could serve as a model for the music that we use in our worship services today?

10. John Piper, *Desiring God: Meditations of a Christian Hedonist*, 2nd ed. (Sisters, OR: Multnomah, 1986), 227.

11. John Piper, *When I Don't Desire God: How to Fight for Joy* (Wheaton, IL: Crossway, 2004), 13, and John Piper, *Desiring God: Meditations of a Christian Hedonist*, 3rd ed. (Sisters, OR: Multnomah, 2003), 18, quoted in Thomas R. Schreiner, "A Biblical Theology of the Glory of God," in *For the Fame of God's Name: Essays in Honor of John Piper*, ed. Sam Storms and Justin Taylor (Wheaton, IL: Crossway, 2010), 234.

5. Summarize the significance of fire in connection with worship.
6. What is different and what is the same about temple worship compared to the worship we experience in the church today?
7. Why should corporate worship be Christ-centered, and how is this reflected in your church's services?

6

FIRE AND RAIN

Mount Carmel: Mountain of Contested Worship

*People manufacture substitutes for God. They make physical
idols as symbols for transcendence, or they make within their
minds counterfeit conceptions of God. The counterfeit conceptions
may be close to the truth. That is the way a counterfeit works.
A counterfeit must be close to the truth in order to seem
plausible. It expresses fragments of the truth about God in
spite of itself, it testifies to God—but in a distorted way.*
—Vern S. Poythress, *Theophany*

My wife and I flew into Tokyo several years ago at the peak of cherry blossom season. Because our trip happened to extend over Easter weekend, we really hoped we could locate a Christian church where we would be able to attend worship and celebrate the resurrection with Japanese believers. Unfortunately, the local telephone directory in our hotel room was not the least bit helpful in my search for a church. (The fact that I was not fluent in reading Japanese may have also been part of the problem.) An internet search also yielded nothing. In desperation, I wandered through the streets to see if I could spot anything resembling a church. In the end, my multiple search methods yielded zilch.

My lack of success wasn't surprising. Some observers estimate that 70 percent of Japanese people claim to be Shintoists and 70 percent claim to be Buddhists. It takes a lot of syncretism to make that math work! Only approximately 1 percent of the population of Japan claims to be Christian. Although it was Easter while we were there, you never would have known that it was a significant Christian holiday.

Our trip to Japan also included a visit to the ancient capital of Kyoto, with its meticulously manicured gardens and traditional teahouses. One of our tour stops was the famous Sanjusangendo Hall, which is located within a Buddhist temple. It was an unforgettable sight. Originally built in AD 1164 at the request of the emperor, the temple remains open to tourists. After removing our shoes at the entrance, we were escorted down a long hallway that led into an enclosed, darkened chamber. Once our eyes had adjusted, we gazed in amazement at one thousand and one golden life-sized statues of Kannon-Bosatsu Buddhas, all of which had been carved during the twelfth and thirteenth centuries. In the center of the long row of images stood the principal image of Kannon, which towered over the others at eleven feet tall. This display of Buddhas was guarded by still more statues of twenty-eight Hindu deities. All these gods were lined up, row upon row upon row. To be honest, it was an eerie experience to be in that darkened room surrounded by a maze of pagan "gods."

No one should be surprised that the worship of images of false deities continues to be very much alive in the twenty-first century—even in the Bible Belt of the southern United States, where I reside. In my southern city, a jade statue of the Buddha arrived recently on a traveling exhibit for the second time. This eight-foot tall, four-ton idol, which was surrounded by offerings of flowers and fruit, attracted an estimated ten thousand visitors.

A leading local newspaper interviewed a woman who had seen the statue six times. She told the reporter, "I just like to be there with it. I can feel the energy."[1]

As may be fairly typical in the United States, my city not only has a large number of churches and synagogues but also a variety of Buddhist centers, a Hindu center that serves more than four thousand Hindu families, at least five Islamic centers, and a Confucius Institute. Where did all of this begin? What are the roots of idolatry and of the alternative deities that are worshipped throughout the world? From Scripture we learn that the worship of false gods started very early and was often associated with mountains and their summits. One early example of this is the contest that took place on the summit of Mount Carmel.

Historical Context

Mount Carmel was the site of an extraordinary event in the history of worship. It did not occur in a vacuum but was part of the historical trail that we have been following in this book. Remember how God had powerfully demonstrated, at two earlier mountains, his worthiness to be worshipped.

At Mount Sinai, Jehovah God had appeared, accompanied by dramatic signs. He had given to Moses the Decalogue, which clearly warned against idolatry and instructed his people to worship him alone: "You shall not make for yourself an image in the form of anything in heaven above or on the earth beneath or in the waters below. You shall not bow down to them or worship them" (Ex. 20:4–5).

Years later, at Jerusalem's Mount Zion, God had appeared in the fullness of his glory at the dedication of Solomon's temple.

1. Quoted in Tim Funk, "Charlotte's Latest Tourist Attraction? A Jade Statue of the Buddha," *The Charlotte Observer*, May 10, 2015, https://www.charlotte observer.com/living/religion/article20636115.html.

The people responded by falling prostrate before him in worship. And they were not worshipping any visual images or statues of God, because, in keeping with the second commandment, the new temple did not contain any. Jehovah had so manifested his presence that the people could not help but worship him.

Sadly, this high point in Israel's history did not sustain God's people and their leaders indefinitely. All was not well during Solomon's forty-year reign from 970–930 BC. Tragically, in his old age Solomon was led astray by foreign wives and followed other gods and even built divinely forbidden worship sites on the Mount of Olives.

How easily God's people and their leaders can be deceived and drawn into false, idolatrous worship! Following King Solomon's death, his son Rehoboam took over the kingdom, then stubbornly refused to lower taxes when asked to do so by the overburdened people. This unwise decision led to a conflict in which the ten northern tribes rebelled against Rehoboam and appointed Jeroboam as their new king. The divided kingdom now consisted of Israel in the north and Judah in the south.

The sixth king to ascend the throne of the northern kingdom of Israel was Ahab, who reigned from 874–853 BC. Every single king of Israel leading up to him had been evil, and Ahab was no exception. It is hard to fathom that the reign of this infamously corrupt king began only about a hundred years after the high point of the dedication of Solomon's temple on Mount Zion. How quickly people turn from the truth! Even a generation or two can make a huge difference.

King Ahab had married a fiery woman named Jezebel—a worshipper of the Phoenician god Baal. Her reputation for evil and violence is well deserved. To please his queen, King Ahab welcomed false prophets of Baal to Israel and built high places for the worship of Baal throughout the land. Scripture tells us that "Ahab did more to provoke the LORD, the God of Israel, to anger than all the kings of Israel who were before him" (1 Kings 16:33 ESV). What an indictment!

During this very dark period of Israel's history, God raised up a feisty prophet named Elijah to announce that the rain in the land would stop. And it wouldn't resume until he said so.

After the prophet made this announcement to the pagan king in a direct, threatening confrontation in the palace, you can imagine that relations between the two were at an all-time low. Elijah really had no choice but to flee for his life. He retreated from the palace and hid out at the remote brook Cherith, where God took care of his needs and provided a unique catering service to deliver his meals—ravens! Eventually the brook dried up, and at the Lord's direction, Elijah moved on to the town of Zarephath. There a widow fed him, and he raised her son from the dead. All of this set the stage for the main event that would define Elijah's life.

Mountaintop Contest

The drought that Elijah had announced had become life-threatening. It was far more severe than the periodic shortages of rain you and I may experience that necessitate a ban on watering our lawns or an embargo on car washes. This was not the third month but the third *year* of no precipitation in Israel. Despite the fact that the drought had not yielded repentance on Ahab's part, God instructed Elijah to present himself before the evil monarch and inform him that God would once again send rain on the land. A face-to-face encounter was arranged.

Scripture gives us a transcript of the gutsy words that Elijah delivered to the king: "I have not made trouble for Israel. . . . But you and your father's family have. You have abandoned the LORD's commands and have followed the Baals. Now summon the people from all over Israel to meet me on Mount Carmel. And bring the four hundred and fifty prophets of Baal and the four hundred prophets of Asherah, who eat at Jezebel's table" (1 Kings 18:18–19).

Notice how the text uses the plural "Baals." This is because there were many Baals who were worshipped in Israel, not just one. During the days of King Ahab, the most prominent Baal was the deity of Tyre, called Baal-melqart. One commentary helpfully explains, "The polytheism of the ancient world was an open system—there was always room for more gods, and if a god was deemed to be active and powerful in the region, it was logical to acknowledge that deity. This was not an issue of theological ideology; it was a matter of practical necessity. People worshipped gods by caring for their needs, such as providing food for them. As a result, the deity would not become angry and the attention he received brought benefits to the people."[2]

Why Choose Mount Carmel?

If you were responsible for organizing an important contest or event, you would want to stage it at the most appropriate site. Some who have read the account of this historical event have questioned why, out of all the possible locations in the land of the Bible, this contest was staged on Mount Carmel. There are several compelling reasons.

A Sacred Space

Temples to Baal and to other pagan shrines were commonly located on mountaintops. It makes sense that a mountain summit would be selected rather than a valley or a lakeside.

---

2. John Monson, commentary on 1 Kings 18:4, in *Zondervan Illustrated Bible Backgrounds Commentary*, ed. John H. Walton, vol. 3, *1 & 2 Kings, 1 & 2 Chronicles, Ezra, Nehemiah, Esther* (Grand Rapids: Zondervan, 2009), 77.

A Ready Supply of Moisture

Mount Carmel in particular is known for its lush vegetation, due to its proximity to the Mediterranean Sea. Westerly winds blowing over the sea pick up moisture and deposit it as they drift over the rising terrain of Carmel. This results in an average rainfall of approximately thirty-two inches a year. Israel as a whole receives less than twenty-five inches annually and sees very little precipitation in the summer. Mount Carmel's high slopes cool efficiently at night, which helps to explain why moist sea air forms dew on the ground of the mountain as many as 250 nights a year. A ready supply of moisture was going to come in handy!

Baal's Home Turf

Baal was known as the god of rain and storms and as the controller of lightning. Fittingly, Elijah chose the most optimum place to give the prophets of Baal a familiar home-field advantage. After all, many ancients believed that deities performed more reliably in certain geographical locations. If Baal's prophets could not produce rain even at Mount Carmel, it would be a devastating blow to Baal, the god of rain, on his home turf.

Baal Fails; Jehovah Wins

The odds were four hundred fifty to one. Elijah was massively outnumbered. To begin the contest, the four hundred fifty prophets of Baal chose two bulls to sacrifice—one for their offering and the other for Elijah's. Would Baal be able to defend his honor and display his power by calling down fire to consume the sacrifice? The stakes were high. As we saw in the last chapter, fire was often used as a visual sign of God's presence among his people. Would Baal be able to duplicate this display of power on demand?

The first attempt failed miserably, but Baal's prophets were persistent. Yet their repeated and desperate attempts, over a period

Visiting Mount Carmel Today

Contrary to what you might envision, Carmel is not just a single peak but a triangular mountain ridge that extends through northern Israel for thirty-one miles. It is located near the modern city of Haifa and adjacent to the Mediterranean Sea. The ancient Egyptians called it "holy headland"—a name that appears in an inscription discovered by archaeologists. It has also been nicknamed "the antelope's nose"—a designation that makes sense when you look at its shape on a physical map or on Google Earth. As far as mountains go, Carmel is not exceptionally high—a mere 1,790 feet.

Perhaps you have had the experience of visiting Mount Carmel as a tourist or a student. A statue of Elijah, wielding a knife, always catches the attention of first-time visitors. It certainly caught mine. On the top of the mountain, across from the statue, stands a Carmelite sanctuary and monastery, which was originally built in the seventeenth century and rebuilt in the mid-nineteenth century. The rooftop observation deck of the monastery provides a panoramic view of the surroundings, which include the Mediterranean Sea. It is the perfect vantage point from which to imagine the scene of the contest between God's prophet and the prophets of Baal.

of many hours, did not yield a single spark. Elijah's humorous quips could not have had a calming effect on the prophets: "Shout louder! . . . Surely he is a god! Perhaps he is deep in thought, or busy, or traveling. Maybe he is sleeping and must be awakened" (1 Kings 18:27). The shouts grew louder, and blood flowed freely as the prophets lacerated themselves with swords and spears. At the end of the day, all this frenzy was for naught. They had been wasting their time from the start.

Finally, with the obvious failure and impotence of Baal on full display, it was time for Elijah to move into action. He began

Fig. 6.1. Statue of Elijah on Mount Carmel

by repairing the altar of the Lord with twelve stones. Then he placed kindling wood on the altar, along with a bull that had already been cut into pieces. In order to make the challenge even more to his disadvantage, he saturated the altar and the sacrifice with water. Three times he poured four jars of water on the altar.

Archaeologists have found Canaanite and Israelite jars from this era that hold over eight gallons of water or wine. Smaller jars held half that. So, at bare minimum, the amount of water that was poured on Elijah's sacrifice would have been 48 gallons.

Then Elijah humbly but confidently prayed, "LORD, the God of Abraham, Isaac and Israel, let it be known today that you are God in Israel and that I am your servant and have done all these things at your command. Answer me, LORD, answer me, so these people will know that you, LORD, are God, and that you are turning their hearts back again" (1 Kings 18:36–37).

God's response was immediate. Video footage of what happened next would have been spectacular. From the Lord came flames of fire that lit up the sacrifice, burning not only the wood but also the bull and the stones, and even licking up the water in the trench.

The message could not have been clearer. All the people fell prostrate to the ground and cried aloud, "The Lord—he is God!" Elijah told the king that rain was on the way. Then, weary but invigorated, Elijah climbed to the top of the mountain and bent toward the ground with his face between his knees. Seven times he told his servant to look toward the Mediterranean Sea for rain. Finally, his servant spotted a small cloud, the size of a man's hand, rising over the sea. It appeared to be drifting toward them.

The sky turned black, and a deluge of rain drenched the ground. The devastating drought of three long years was over— and certainly not because of the action of the reputed god of rain and storms. The superiority of Jehovah over Baal was no longer in question. Meanwhile Ahab, wishing to get off the mountain ASAP, jumped into his chariot and raced ahead to the town of Jezreel. Amazingly, Elijah was able to run ahead of Ahab's chariot as it descended the mountain. Was this a supernatural infusion of adrenaline? Elijah did not have long to catch his breath, however, because when Queen Jezebel learned of the defeat of the prophets of Baal on Mount Carmel, she was more determined than ever to polish off the prophet.

Once again, Elijah was on the run. This time he fled to the southernmost town of Israel, Beersheba. This would have been almost a hundred-mile trek, and probably on foot, but the threat on his life left him no choice. In Beersheba, Elijah said goodbye to his servant and traveled, alone and discouraged, farther south into the Sinai desert.

Eventually Elijah arrived at Horeb, the mountain of God— also known as Mount Sinai. The God who had earlier appeared to Moses on that very mountain was about to make himself known again on the same peak—this time to Elijah. The journey that had begun earlier at Mount Carmel had now reached Mount Sinai. In an upcoming chapter of this book, we will see that Elijah reappears on yet another mountain. But we'll leave that story for later.

The Ongoing Struggle of True Worship versus Idol Worship

It is hard to comprehend why the dramatic events at Mount Carmel did not result in a permanent turning of the nation back to the exclusive worship of Jehovah. The radical pervasiveness of sin is the only explanation. It's like trying to eradicate crabgrass from your lawn. Sadly, a few years later there were still enough Baal worshippers in the land to fill a Baal temple.

Following the death of Ahab, Jehu ascended to the throne as Israel's king.

Then Jehu brought all the people together and said to them, "Ahab served Baal a little; Jehu will serve him much. Now summon all the prophets of Baal, all his servants and all his priests. See that no one is missing, because I am going to hold a great sacrifice for Baal. Anyone who fails to come will no longer live." But Jehu was acting deceptively in order to destroy the servants of Baal. (2 Kings 10:18–19).

It worked. The prophets, priests, and servants of Baal filled the temple. The Baal worshippers who came out of the woodwork paid for it with their lives. In the end, King Jehu demolished the temple of Baal and turned it into a latrine. Good for him! But he didn't go far enough. 2 Kings 10:29 reports that "he did not turn away from the sins of Jeroboam son of Nebat, which he had caused Israel to commit—the worship of the golden calves at Bethel and Dan." Another form of idolatrous false worship continued to thrive. Polytheism and idolatry remained alive and well in Israel.

Application for Today

To what extent does idolatry impact our worship today? Let me explain what I mean by "idolatry." The main Greek term that is used for *idolatry* in the New Testament is *eidololatria*—a compound consisting of two words. The first word, *eidolo*, means "what is seen." The second, *latria*, means "to serve or worship." So idolatry refers to serving or worshipping someone or something that has a visible form. Jesus's charge to "pray to your Father, who is unseen" (Matt. 6:6) is a reminder to us that we must never pray to visible idols. The apostle Paul wrote that "what is seen is temporary, but what is unseen is eternal" (2 Cor. 4:18). Because Christianity centers on the invisible God, we must constantly guard against worshipping objects that are visible. Author James Aughey reminds us, "As a weak limb grows stronger by exercise, so will your faith be strengthened by the very efforts you make in stretching it out toward things unseen."[3]

Humans are incurably religious and must worship something

3. John H. Aughey, *Spiritual Gems of the Ages* (Cincinnati, 1886), 95.

or someone. In Romans 1, the apostle Paul warns about the human tendency to worship idols. John Calvin insightfully reinforced this truth when he wrote, "Man's nature, so to speak, is a perpetual factory of idols."[4] Calvin understood that all forms of idolatry siphon off the glory that belongs exclusively to our Creator and Redeemer. At the root of our human problem is an unwillingness to glorify God and give him the central place in our lives. "Although they knew God, they neither glorified him as God nor gave thanks to him, but their thinking became futile and their foolish hearts were darkened" (Rom. 1:21). We prefer to glorify ourselves. It's not hard to see how this impacts our worship.

A New God for a New Era?

I was surprised recently to come across a rather novel, but blatant, outcropping of idolatry. Anticipating the time when machines will outsmart and control humans, former Google tech mogul Anthony Levandowski has created an artificial intelligence–based god. His purpose? "To develop and promote the realization of a Godhead based on artificial intelligence and through understanding and worship of the Godhead contribute to the betterment of society."* Let that sink in.

* Quoted in Olivia Solon, "Deus ex Machina: Former Google Engineer Is Developing an AI God," *The Guardian*, September 28, 2017, https://www.the guardian.com/technology/2017/sep/28/artificial-intelligence-god-anthony -levandowski.

Writer and university instructor David Foster Wallace gave a memorable commencement address at Kenyon College in 2005. In this address he asserted that "there is no such thing as not

---

4. John Calvin, *Institutes of the Christian Religion*, ed. John T. McNeill, trans. Ford Lewis Battles, vol. 1 (Louisville: Westminster John Knox Press, 1960), 1.11.8.

worshipping. Everybody worships. The only choice we get is what to worship. And the compelling reason for maybe choosing some sort of God . . . is that pretty much anything else you worship will eat you alive."[5] Why do people choose other gods? Sometimes because their thinking has been distorted by a lie. At the base of their personality is a false belief system that is centered on an idol—that is, the belief that something besides God can give us the life and joy that only God can give. "They exchanged the truth about God for a lie," Paul writes (Rom. 1:25). Tim Keller develops this thought in his book *Counterfeit Gods*: "A counterfeit god is anything so central and essential to your life that, should you lose it, your life would feel hardly worth living."[6] Does anything in your life come to mind that might be described as a counterfeit god? The challenge of Elijah that echoed on the mountaintop needs to be heard today as well: "How long will you waver between two opinions? If the LORD is God, follow him" (1 Kings 18:21).

It's no surprise that the New Testament frequently condemns idolatry, which takes glory and worship away from God. Idolatry is an enemy of God-centered worship. Consider these New Testament warnings:

No immoral, impure or greedy person—such a person is an idolater—has any inheritance in the kingdom of Christ and of God. (Eph. 5:5)

Put to death, therefore, whatever belongs to your earthly nature: sexual immorality, impurity, lust, evil desires and greed, which is idolatry. (Col. 3:5)

---

5. Available online at "Transcription of the 2005 Kenyon Commencement Address—May 21, 2005," Purdue University, accessed July 10, 2019, https://web.ics.purdue.edu/~drkelly/DFWKenyonAddress2005.pdf.

6. Timothy Keller, *Counterfeit Gods: The Empty Promises of Money, Sex, and Power, and the Only Hope That Matters* (New York: Penguin Books, 2011), xviii.

Their destiny is destruction, their god is their stomach, and their glory is in their shame. (Phil. 3:19)

Flee from idolatry. (1 Cor. 10:14)

Dear children, keep yourselves from idols. (1 John 5:21)

How do we keep ourselves from idols? Tim Keller gives this wise counsel: when we succumb to idolatry, we may actually be saying, "Lord, it's good to have you, but there's this other thing I must have, without which life is not happy or meaningful. If I can't have it, I will despair. You are not enough. I need this too, as a requirement for being fulfilled. In fact, if you would take it from me, I'd turn my back on you, for you are negotiable but this is not! This is the real goal of my life—if you are not useful to me in achieving it, I might turn away from you."[7] Ouch. Idols aren't always visible, but they can nevertheless dwell in our hearts.

It should be an ongoing prayer concern for all believers to unmask the idols in their lives. Do not let idols rob you of your joy in God's presence. You and I were made for God-centered worship. It is in worshipping God alone that we find our supreme delight and satisfaction. The Mount Carmel contest is a good reminder of this.

Questions for Reflection and Discussion

1. Can you think of any examples of idol worship that hit close to home for you?
2. What might be some reasons why Mount Carmel was chosen for the contest with the prophets of Baal?

---

7. Timothy Keller, *Romans 1–7 For You* (Purcellville, VA: The Good Book Company, 2014), 195.

3. What do we know about Baal worship from Scripture and other sources?
4. What do we learn about prayer from 1 Kings 18?
5. What were some of the results of Elijah's victory over Baal?
6. What happened among God's people in the days of Jehu?
7. What does the New Testament teach about idolatry, and how does that teaching apply to our worship? How can we resist idolatry that would harm our worship?

Part 3

CLIMBING
SUMMITS
IN THE NEW
COVENANT

7

THIRST QUENCHER

Mount Gerizim: Mountain
of Samaritan Worship

*It might happen once in a while that something I said or wrote was
sufficiently heeded for me to persuade myself that it represented a
serious impact on our time. . . . I beg you to believe me, multiply
these tiny triumphs by a million, add them all together, and
they are nothing—less than nothing, a positive impediment—
measured against one draught of that living water Christ offers
to the spiritually thirsty, irrespective of who or what they are.*
—Malcolm Muggeridge, *Jesus Rediscovered*

Have you ever had the adrenaline-pumping experience of viewing
a telecast or video clip of a major United States political party
convention during a presidential election year? Typically, the
party nominee who is slated to run for president steps onto the
stage amid raucous fanfare, thunderous applause, and earsplitting
music. Participants who do not succumb to migraine headaches
can be seen raising their hands in "adoration" and exuding a warm
emotional glow. Some have likened these events to what happens
when Christian believers gather for worship. Could there be any
truth to this?

Sit in a football stadium as your favorite hometown team scores a touchdown, and you'll see evidence of hero worship—to say nothing of what you see in the halftime shows at the Super Bowl. Attend a concert by the latest popular musical group, and you'll see raised hands and looks of ecstasy on the faces of many fans. Yes, not all worship takes place in church. Author and pastor Tim Keller has posted, "You don't get to decide to worship. Everyone worships something. The only choice you get is what [or who] to worship."[1]

So far we have climbed three mountains with worship in mind. The Mount Sinai, Mount Zion, and Mount Carmel events were all set within old covenant history. In this chapter we will transition to the New Testament and discover how the coming of Christ significantly changed worship. You'll recall that a unifying metaphor or theme has guided our travel, which can be illustrated in figure 7.1.

To summarize briefly: we learned that in the garden of Eden the first couple enjoyed God's immediate presence, because God himself had chosen to dwell with them. But as a consequence of their fall into sin, Adam and Eve, and all of us who are sons of Adam and daughters of Eve, were banished from the garden. God then announced the *protoevangelium* in Genesis 3:15, promising that he would come in the form of a Messiah. Eventually the Lord would restore the garden in the new earth and heaven.

Moving closer toward that end, the invisible God took on a visible, localized presence in the form of Christ in first-century Israel. Instead of the visible glory cloud of the Old Testament, the second person of the Godhead assumed a unique incarnate physical appearance. "Christ as the permanent 'theophany' surpasses

---

1. Timothy Keller (@timkellernyc), Twitter, February 2, 2015, 8:05 a.m., https://twitter.com/timkellernyc/status/562280568109678592?lang=en.

any one appearance of God in the Old Testament, and he also surpasses them even when they are all taken together."[2]

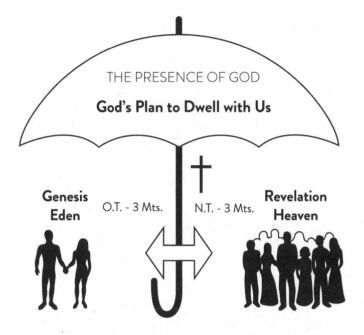

Fig. 7.1. Umbrella: God's Visible, Localized Presence in History

A Conversation with a Potential Worshipper

Many key events and conversations from Christ's life on earth are recorded in one or more of the four gospels. In this chapter we will single out a conversation that Jesus had with a woman who became an unlikely worshipper of the true God. Her story is recorded only in the gospel of John.

What circumstances precipitated this encounter? The apostle

2. Vern S. Poythress, *Theophany: A Biblical Theology of God's Appearing* (Wheaton, IL: Crossway, 2018), 308.

John writes that Jesus "*had* to go through Samaria" (John 4:4). Why would he say that? At this point in history, the animosity that existed between Jews and Samaritans was almost palpable. Most Jews avoided setting foot on Samaritan soil, even though the road through Samaria was the most direct route between Judea and Galilee. Rather than risk a face-to-face encounter with a mixed-race Samaritan, Jews would willingly trek approximately twenty-five extra miles in order to circumvent Samaria—perhaps making the journey twice as long. Not Jesus. He deliberately chose the direct and shorter route.

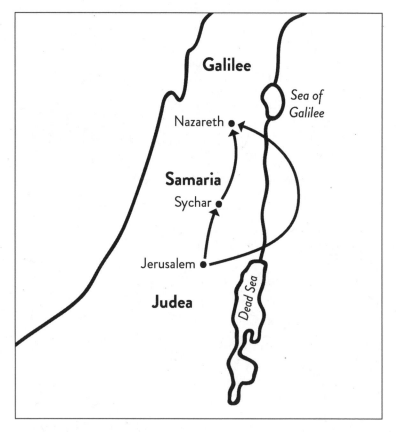

Fig. 7.2. Map: Avoiding Samaria

His decision was clearly not just a matter of geographical preference. It was all part of God's providence. Jesus said, "My food . . . is to do the will of him who sent me and to finish his work" (v. 34). His life and ministry were always in sync with the Spirit. His meeting with the Samaritan woman was far from a coincidental encounter. It was a divine appointment.

Crossing Three Important Barriers

Christ's conversation with the woman from Samaria effectively crossed three important barriers.

A Gender Barrier

Men in that culture would not have been seen talking with a woman in public. But Jesus did just that. In fact, he initiated the conversation as the woman approached the well. This comes as no surprise. Throughout his public ministry, Christ often showed concern for the status and treatment of women. From Jesus's perspective, this woman had as much potential to become a true worshipper as any man had.

A Racial Barrier

When Jesus addressed her, the Samaritan woman pointed out the problem with his doing so: "You are a Jew and I am a Samaritan woman." As John's gospel then explains, "Jews do not associate with Samaritans" (John 4:9). The roots of this animosity went back hundreds of years, to the period of history in which the Assyrian armies conquered the northern kingdom of Israel. Following their conquest, some of the Assyrian men settled in the new land in the area of Samaria. As you might expect, they fell in love with the local Jewish women. The mixed marriages of Jews and pagan Gentiles produced the mixed ethnicity of the Samaritans, which led to social tensions in first-century Israel.

But the barriers between Jews and Samaritans were offensive to Jesus.

A Social Barrier

The Samaritan woman had a shady past. Her lifestyle indicated that she was spiritually dead. She had been married five times and was currently living with a man to whom she was not married. The rabbis in that day generally disapproved of anyone entering more than three marriages in a lifetime, even if their spouses had died. But what made this woman's situation even more problematic was the fact that she had a live-in boyfriend.

It appears that her reputation preceded her—at least in her local community. The text tells us that this conversation between Jesus and the woman from Samaria occurred at noon—the time of day when the sun would have been most direct and intense. In that Middle Eastern culture, women made every effort to come to the well during the cooler times of the day, such as early morning or evening, and often in groups—not alone. Some commentators have suggested that she was a shunned woman who deliberately chose to come to the well at a time when she was least likely to encounter the scorn of other women. It appears that Jesus recognized the potential in this particular woman to become a worshipper of the true God and sought her out.

An Unexpected Answer to a Human Thirst

The biblical account in John 4 records an exchange of questions and answers between Jesus and the woman. His initial question establishes a conversational bridge: "Will you give me a drink?" (v. 7). Undoubtedly, the woman was surprised by Jesus's request. As a Jew, Jesus would be considered ceremonially unclean if he even so much as touched a drinking vessel that a Samaritan had handled.

What to Know about Jacob's Well

It is possible, though perhaps a little risky, to visit the site of Jacob's well today. The well itself is located in what was once called the city of Sychar, which is now part of the West Bank. If you are so inclined, there is a shop on the site where friendly people will happily sell you water that has been drawn from Jacob's well.

In the fourth century, Byzantine Christians erected a church over the well, and by the twelfth century, the Crusaders had replaced it with a church of their own. The footprint of this Crusader church became the exact location for a modern Greek Orthodox church that was completed in 2007. If you visit this site today, you will see a small chapel that contains the actual well. The opening at the top of the well is seven and a half feet wide. Current estimates report that it's around sixty-seven feet deep, although in the first century it would probably have been much deeper.

Typically, a major well would have a large donut-shaped capstone with a small hole in the center for lowering a bucket. The capstone would keep dirt from blowing into the well and prevent children from falling into the shaft. It would also provide a surface on which to place objects or to sit. Jesus would have been sitting on the capstone of the well as the woman approached.

How could the woman not have been confused when the man before her offered to give her "living" water? She may at first have thought in merely physical terms. Was Jesus speaking of some "magic" water that would eliminate the backbreaking work of drawing water on a daily basis? In that day, cisterns and most wells were filled with stagnant water, in contrast with flowing springs that provided fresh or living water. Jesus's surprising offer of living water eventually led the woman to ask for some of the water that only Christ could give.

In the course of the conversation, Jesus revealed his divine identity as the promised Messiah. When the truth sank in, the woman was unable to contain her joy. The good news was too good to keep to herself. By the end of the day, many of the Samaritans in the village of Sychar, along with the woman, had been transformed into true worshippers.

A Series of Instructions about Worship

The conversation between Jesus and the Samaritan woman took an unexpected turn when he began to inquire about her past husbands and the man with whom she was living now. Perhaps feeling uncomfortable, she abruptly shifted the conversation away from her past sexual history and onto the subject of worship. In response to her diversionary tactics, Christ took the opportunity to provide some helpful teaching about worship, perhaps recognizing that her initiative in raising a question about the subject hinted at her potential to become a true worshipper. Interestingly, ten out of the thirteen times that the word *worship* appears in the entire gospel of John are packed into these few verses.

Let's take a look at several important principles that can be drawn from what Jesus taught the Samaritan woman.

Our Worship Is Not Restricted by Location (vv. 19–21)

The woman started by asking which of two competing mountains, Mount Gerizim or Mount Zion, was the proper place to worship. There was a story and a lot of history behind the question.

If you were to visit Jacob's well today, you would see on the near horizon a mountain named Gerizim, which rises 2,900 feet above sea level, along with a nearby twin mountain called Mount Ebal. This area is part of what is now called the West Bank, and a town named Nablus is located there—one of the oldest cities in the world. Years earlier, Joshua, having entered the promised

Fig. 7.3. Location of Jacob's Well between Mounts Gerizim and Ebal

land, had gathered the thousands of Israelites at the base of these two mountains (see Josh. 8:30–35). There, following Moses's instructions from Deuteronomy 27:11–26, he would have had the Levites read the law antiphonally—both its blessings and curses. This part of the Samaritans' homeland became a revered place to those who remembered this historic event.

After the Jews returned from captivity in Babylon, the Samaritans built a temple for worship on Mount Gerizim, modeling it after Solomon's temple. They believed that Moses had designated this mountain for the temple's location rather than Mount Zion in Jerusalem. They also believed that Mount Gerizim, rather than Jerusalem, was the site of Abraham's aborted sacrifice of his beloved son Isaac. The foundations of the Samaritan temple can be viewed today on top of Mount Gerizim, under the ruins of a Byzantine church and monastery. An oil lamp that is displayed in the Israel Museum in Jerusalem depicts a temple and altar on Mount Gerizim.

What happened to that temple? Around 127 BC, one of the Jewish Hasmonean kings, John Hyrcanus, led soldiers to Mount Gerizim to destroy the temple. The king believed that Jerusalem should be the place of worship rather than Gerizim. But even after the temple was demolished and burned by fire, the Samaritans continued to worship on the site. Samaritans to this day sacrifice lambs at their annual Passover festival at the summit of Mount Gerizim, believing that this is the one and only holy place for worship.

The Samaritans tried to settle the score a few years after the destruction of their temple. Josephus wrote, "When Coponius was procurator of Judea, the following incident occurred. The Jews were celebrating the Feast of Unleavened Bread (which we call Passover). It was customary during that season for the priests to open the temple gates just after midnight. But on this occasion when the gates were first opened, some Samaritans came privately into Jerusalem and threw some human corpses into the temple cloisters. As a result the Jews then banned the Samaritans from the temple, even though they had not previously done this at such festivals."[3] Tensions seemed to only escalate between the Jews and the Samaritans!

More than one hundred years after the temple's destruction, the Samaritan woman faced Jesus, asking him to tell her the proper location for worship. It made perfect sense that this question would have loomed large in her thinking. Jesus answered with these surprising words: "Believe me, a time is coming when you will worship the Father neither on this mountain nor in Jerusalem" (John 4:21). Instead of getting trapped into choosing one of the two mountains, Jesus said in effect, "Neither mountain." The time of his death and resurrection was fast approaching and

3. Josephus, *Antiquities of the Jews*, bk. 18, chap. 2.2, in *The Works of Josephus: Complete and Unabridged*, new updated ed., trans. William Whiston (Peabody, MA: Hendrickson Publishers, 1987).

would mark the end of Jerusalem's being the special location for worship. Ultimately, even the Jerusalem temple would not prove to be indestructible. It was leveled to the ground by an invasion of Roman soldiers in AD 70.

From that time on, God's people have understood that it is not his plan to designate special holy sites for worship. Jesus is present wherever his people assemble to call on his name. The important thing is not *where* we worship but *who* and *how* we worship.

Our Worship Should Be Supported by a Proper Understanding of Biblical Truth (v. 22)

Jesus also tells the woman, "You Samaritans worship what you do not know; we worship what we do know, for salvation is from the Jews." The Samaritans accepted only the first five books of the Old Testament. They used their own revised translation of the Pentateuch but did not believe or use the other Old Testament historical books, prophets, or poetic books. It would not have been possible for the Samaritans to worship God properly, because their understanding of worship was truncated at best. It was not based on the entire canon of Old Testament Scripture.

Our Worship Should Have a God-Centered Focus (v. 23)

Jesus continues, "A time is coming and has now come when the true worshipers will worship the Father in the Spirit and in truth, for they are the kind of worshipers the Father seeks." God the Father, the Creator and King of the universe, actively seeks our worship. That is amazing, and it is true!

In all too many churches, the main focus of worship is wrongly placed on the felt needs of the congregation, or on the people up front, rather than on God himself. This worship can be described as human-centered. But the focus of our worship should be on the triune God. This means that our prayers should be addressed to God, our singing should be directed to him, and our offerings should be presented to him. God in turn speaks to us through the preaching and teaching of his Word. This is the rhythm of God-centered worship. The great divide in some quarters of the Christian community is not formal vs. informal or contemporary vs. traditional worship but God-centered vs. man-centered worship.

Our Worship Ought to Be in Spirit and in Truth (v. 24)

Finally Jesus says, "God is spirit, and his worshipers must worship in the Spirit and in truth." Many church attenders would easily recognize this passage but would be hard-pressed to explain it. Let's take a closer look.

The Greek language does not distinguish between uppercase and lowercase letters. This means it is impossible for us to know whether the word *spirit* should be translated into English as "spirit" or as "Spirit."[4] If the word *spirit* is translated with a lowercase *s*, some commentators understand this to mean that our human spirit should be engaged in worship. This view seems to reflect Matthew 15:8, where Jesus said of the Pharisees, "These people honor me with their lips, but their hearts are far from me." Outward physical motions are not enough. True worship happens when our spirits are fully engaged.

But let's be real. I suspect that not a single reader of this book can truthfully say that they have never lost their focus in a service of worship. We are all too familiar with the myriad distractions that compete for our attention: lab test results that are due on Monday morning, a harsh word that we exchanged with a fellow employee, a traffic ticket that we didn't deserve, the obnoxious perfume that someone near us is wearing. Not to mention the alerts on our phones! With all these distractions, our bodies may

---

4. Note that the NIV translation of John 4:24 chooses to use "the Spirit" whereas the ESV and most other versions translate it as "spirit."

find it easy to go through the outward motions of worship while our inner spirits fail to be engaged.

Some commentators suggest that the word *spirit* refers not exclusively to our human spirit but to both the human spirit and the Holy Spirit simultaneously. Thus the indwelling presence of the Holy Spirit motivates and enables us to offer whole-person worship that engages our innermost spirit.

Yet other commentators believe that *Spirit* refers exclusively to the Holy Spirit—the third person of the Trinity. In the context of this verse, Jesus affirms that "God is spirit," supporting the view that worshipping in spirit refers to the indwelling Holy Spirit, who enables us to engage in worship. The view that Jesus is referring to the Holy Spirit rather than to the human spirit appears to be supported by other Scriptures as well. For example, in Philippians 3:3 we are told to "worship by the Spirit of God" (ESV).[5] The Holy Spirit is the one who empowers and energizes our worship.

Jesus also instructs us to worship in truth. What does that mean? To worship in truth means to avoid worship that is false and forbidden in Scripture. The moral law in Exodus 20:3–5 reminds us that "You shall have no other gods before me. You shall not make for yourself an image. . . . You shall not bow down to them or worship them." True worship takes these commands seriously.

Worshipping in truth also means that God's people should worship in reality rather than in types and shadows. Jesus uses the same word *truth* when he says, "I am the way and the truth and the life. No one comes to the Father except through me" (John 14:6). In the Old Testament, God's people worshipped with types and shadows that included the tabernacle, the temple, and the sacrificial offerings that were required in that period of

---

5. Ephesians 2:18 indirectly refers to worship when it assures us that "through him [Christ] we both have access to the Father by one Spirit."

redemptive history. All those types and shadows pointed ahead to Jesus Christ. Now that Christ has come, we no longer worship using types and shadows but can come directly to Jesus Christ and offer him true worship.

Later in John's gospel, Jesus says, "Your word is truth" (John 17:17). From this text we can conclude that to worship in truth is to offer worship that is consistent with the truths of Scripture.

Ending of the Story

The woman from Samaria's excitement about her encounter with Jesus led to a village-transforming experience of evangelism explosion. While she transformed her whole village by word of mouth, today, with the communication tools we have available, this might have happened on an even larger scale, through a report on the news or through social media. If this newsworthy encounter had taken place in the twenty-first century, a reporter would soon have appeared to thrust a microphone in front of the woman as a camera operator captured the footage. "Can you tell me what the Teacher said to you? What was it about the conversation you had with Jesus that had such an impact on your village? Did the Teacher have anything controversial to say about worship?" But, while it didn't happen on such a large scale, Jesus's encounter with the woman from Samaria had a happy ending. It was a divine appointment, not a chance meeting, with a woman who was transformed into a true worshipper.

In the fourth century, Ephrem the Syrian, a respected theologian and writer of over four hundred hymns and some commentaries, wrote a moving description of the Samaritan woman's encounter with Jesus. "At the beginning of the conversation he [Jesus] did not make himself known to her, but first she caught sight of a thirsty man, then a Jew, then a Rabbi, afterwards a prophet, last of all the Messiah. She tried to get the better of the thirsty man, she showed dislike of the Jew, she heckled the Rabbi, she was swept off her feet by the prophet, and she adored the Christ."[6] How like God to choose the lowly and lonely of this world to display his amazing love and grace. It was God's plan from the beginning that this shamed woman would be transformed into a worshipper of the true God.

Whenever I think about Jesus's encounter at the base of Mount Gerizim, my mind goes to the famous Beatles song "Eleanor Rigby." Its lyrics tell the story of a lonely woman who died in obscurity and was soon forgotten. Not a single person bothered to attend her funeral.

You and I rub shoulders every day with people like Eleanor Rigby—lonely people like the Samaritan woman who have the potential to become true worshippers. Are you willing to pray that God will use your life to add to the worldwide company of worshippers? What if this means we have to cross some barriers ourselves?

Questions for Reflection and Discussion

1. Do you agree or disagree with Tim Keller's statement "You don't get to decide to worship. Everyone worships something"? Give some examples.
2. What does it mean when John 4 says of Jesus that "he had to go through Samaria"?
3. Jesus crossed gender, racial, and social barriers by talking to the Samaritan woman. What are some examples of how we may cross the same kinds of barriers?

6. Quoted in J. Alexander Findley, *The Fourth Gospel: An Expository Commentary* (London: Epworth Press, 1956), 61, quoted in George R. Beasley-Murray, *John*, Word Biblical Commentary 36 (Waco: Word Books, 1987), 66, quoted in Kenneth E. Bailey, *Jesus Through Middle Eastern Eyes: Cultural Studies in the Gospels* (Downers Grove, IL: IVP Academic, 2008), 215.

4. How would you summarize what Jesus taught the Samaritan woman about worship?

5. Is the typical worship service in your church God-centered? How can churches foster this? Give examples.

6. Explain in your own words what you think it means to worship in spirit and in truth.

7. How can we reach out to the lonely Eleanor Rigbys of our world? Give examples.

8

WINDS OF CHANGE

Interlude: Synagogue Worship

*If enjoying God and being in the presence of God is the
highest purpose for which I exist, then worship and biblical
meditation are not low priorities but high priorities, they
are worthy of my best time, energy and focused attention.*
—John Jefferson Davis, *Meditation and Communion with God*

One of the oldest known synagogues in the land of the Bible is
located at the Gamla Nature Reserve on the Golan Heights.[1] On
one of our trips to Israel, my wife and I set out to find it. Wearing
sturdy hiking boots, we trekked across open fields, down a treacherous rocky path, and finally up some challenging hills until we
arrived at the site. Although the raw beauty of the location was
stunning, what excited us was knowing that this ancient synagogue had existed during Christ's Galilean ministry.

While visiting the synagogue at Gamla, we sat inside its rectangular foundations on the steps that had functioned as seats

---

1. Other first-century synagogues have been uncovered by archaeologists at
Capernaum, Masada, and the Herodium.

Heroism at Gamla

During the first Jewish Revolt in AD 67, the Roman general Vespasian attacked Gamla with his troops and carried out a months-long siege against the village. Josephus, the Jewish historian, reported the tragic story of how four thousand Jews were left dying in the streets after thousands of Roman soldiers charged through the village, in addition to some five thousand who were trampled to death or leaped to their deaths from the summit on which Gamla was located in order to avoid being captured as slaves.* Archaeologists have discovered a thousand catapult stones and even more than a thousand arrowheads in this area, which are all reminders of this devastating war. In modern Israel, Gamla has become not only an important tourist site but also a symbol of heroism. The slogan "Gamla will not fall again" has become a catchphrase to mean that the control of the Golan Heights is critical to the security of Israel. Israelis sometimes refer to Gamla as the "Masada of the North." The story of Masada's fall in AD 73 is a similar drama that took place on an isolated summit and was also part of the Jewish Revolt against the Roman military machine.

*See Josephus, *The Wars of the Jews*, bk. 4, chap. 1.10, in *The Works of Josephus: Complete and Unabridged*, new updated ed., trans. William Whiston (Peabody, MA: Hendrickson Publishers, 1987).

for worshippers. We noted a niche in the corner of the building that at one time had contained the holy scrolls of Scripture. Our knowledgeable guide helped us to imagine what these ruins would have looked like in Christ's day—and perhaps even *to* Christ, if he worshipped in this synagogue. It's true that the Gospels don't record that Jesus visited Gamla, but since we know that he visited numerous synagogues in the area of Galilee, it's very possible that he taught in this location.

Fig. 8.1. Ruins of the Synagogue at Gamla

Transition Away from the Temple

Thus far in our journey through the Bible, we have traced the trajectory of worship locations from the beginning in the garden, to family altars that were presided over by the patriarchs, to Mount Sinai, to the tabernacle, and then to the temple that was built by Solomon on Mount Zion. In this chapter, our focus moves away from the temple and mountains to new locations and forms of worship, starting with the synagogue.

Many Christians know little about synagogue worship. Even my own exposure to synagogue worship was minimal until quite recently, when I stepped out of my comfort zone in order to gain some firsthand knowledge of present-day synagogue worship. One Saturday afternoon, my wife and I attended a synagogue service in close proximity to our home. As outside observers, we took seats toward the back of the room and tried to absorb and process as much as possible. Yes, we recognized some parallels to our own church worship services, but we also observed forms of worship that were not at all familiar to us. Not surprisingly, the physical structure of the building bore little resemblance to the synagogues in several archaeological sites we had visited in Israel.

The Beginnings of Synagogues

How did the practice of worship in synagogues, such as those in Gamla and elsewhere in the land, originate? Here's what we know. In 586 BC the Babylonian armies led by Nebuchadnezzar swept down on Jerusalem, destroying the temple that had been erected during Solomon's reign. The Babylonians managed to capture large numbers of Jewish men, women, and children, and they took them as prisoners of war and transported them back to the city of Babylon, which was located not far from modern Baghdad. Away from their familiar homeland and temple, God's people longed for the experience of corporate worship—especially on festival days and Sabbaths. Some scholars believe that it was during that period of captivity that the Jewish people first began meeting in small groups within homes in order to worship.

How did this practice of gathering for corporate worship transition beyond the context of the Jews' captivity in Babylon? We know that, after seventy long years, the Jewish hostages were finally released from Babylonian captivity and allowed to return to their homeland. Some of those who were in the habit of meeting in small groups wished to continue the practice, especially since worship in the Jerusalem temple was no longer an option. Even after a smaller, less elaborate temple was built by Zerubbabel, traveling to Jerusalem for festivals required more effort and planning than going to a local synagogue did. Over time, the temple declined in its significance as a place for worship.

As synagogue worship gradually replaced temple worship, the people constructed new synagogues throughout the land. In New Testament times, these synagogues served not only as places of teaching and worship but also as law courts, schools, libraries, and marketplaces. The synagogue was often built in the centrally located market square of a town. They became so plentiful that by the time Jesus's ministry began, most towns in Galilee had their own synagogues. The word *synagogue* appears over thirty times in the Gospels and turns up frequently as part of early church history in the book of Acts.

What role did synagogues play in Jesus's life and ministry? Matthew indicates that "Jesus went throughout Galilee, teaching in their synagogues" (4:23; see also Mark 1:39). A further important clue is found in Luke: "He was teaching in their synagogues, and everyone praised him. He went to Nazareth, where he had been brought up, and on the Sabbath day he went into the synagogue, as was his custom" (4:15–16).[2]

Five Evidences of the Essential Role of Scripture in Synagogue Worship

The oldest New Testament description of Jewish synagogue worship is the account in Luke's gospel in which Jesus visits the synagogue in his hometown of Nazareth.[3] At that time Nazareth was a small village covering only about four acres, whereas today it's a significant city that approaches 100,000 residents. The big central idea that comes out of Luke's description of worship in

---

2. Some commentators point out that this same phrase, "as was his custom," is used of the apostle Paul to indicate his own regular synagogue attendance (see Acts 17:2).

3. Today a church is erected over the probable site of the Nazareth synagogue, which is located not far from the old market. Christians have been visiting this spot since the sixth century.

the Nazareth synagogue is that Jesus models the centrality of Scripture in corporate worship gatherings. Sacrificial animal offerings on altars, as had occurred in the temple, seem to have had no place in the synagogues. ·

Christian worship services carry a long tradition of being word-centered. This was also true of synagogue worship. In addition to prayers, first-century synagogue worship included the reading of Scripture, followed by a sermon that explained the meaning of the passage that was read.

Amidst the gravitational pull of our culture away from words and toward images, Christ's use of the words of Scripture in the synagogue emphasize that God's Word must be paramount in our assemblies of worship. Look with me at five pieces of evidence of this, which date back to first-century synagogue worship.

Showcasing Scripture

The main article of furniture in early synagogues was a small chest that contained scrolls of the Hebrew text of the Old Testament, which made the centrality of Scripture visibly and immediately evident. The chest was usually elevated and had stairs leading up to it.

You'll recall that, for a time, both the tabernacle and the temple housed the ark of the covenant, which contained tablets bearing the words of the Old Testament moral law. Among the ruins of the synagogue at Capernaum, archaeologists have discovered a carving of the ark of the covenant, which illustrates the link between the ark and the chest that was used in the synagogue. The Jewish worshippers at Capernaum would have been reminded of connections with the tabernacle and temple, in the past, as they viewed the ark of the covenant in the stone carvings of their synagogue.

Because the scrolls bore the divine name of God, they were highly valued and could never be destroyed. Early synagogues had

---

Scripture through the Years

In the days before there were bound books, the Hebrew Bible was written on small sheets of papyrus and, later, parchment and then glued together in scroll form. As many as twenty sheets might be glued together to form a scroll, which would extend up to twenty feet long or more. In Luke 4:17, the English word "scroll" is translated from the Greek word *biblion*. Sheets of papyrus were made from the stem of the biblios papyrus plant. It is also from the Greek word *biblios* that we derive the word "Bible."

You can imagine that these early scrolls of Scripture were cumbersome to carry. In time, people developed an altered format called a *codex*, in which pages were folded and fastened together on one side. These seem to have replaced scrolls around the second century. Eventually, covers were added to protect the bound sheets, thus evolving into the book format as we know it today.

---

a place called the *genizah,* in the cellar or attic, where worn and frayed parchment scrolls were preserved long after they could be used in worship.

Caring for Sacred Scrolls

Scripture was so central to synagogue worship that synagogues employed a *hazzan*—an attendant whose primary responsibility was to care for the sacred scrolls (see Luke 4:20). In some synagogues, the *hazzan* wore many hats. In addition to his primary responsibility of caring for the sacred scrolls, he might oversee the cleaning of the building and the teaching of the children. In later years, the *hazzan* became the chief singer—or, in today's language, a cantor. It was his job to blow three blasts on the trumpet from the roof of the synagogue to announce the beginning and end of the Sabbath.

Reading Scripture Repeatedly in Worship

Some commentators have suggested there may have been as many as seven Scripture readings in a single service of synagogue worship. Our knowledge about the typical format of synagogue services is derived from ancient Jewish sources such as the Mishnah—the Jewish codification of the oral law. Below is the order of service that was the likely pattern of synagogue worship. Note its strong emphasis on God's Word.

1. A reading of Deuteronomy 6:4–5 (which is known as the *Shema*), followed by prayers of thanksgiving
2. Prayer with congregation ("amen" response)
3. Reading from the Pentateuch
4. Reading from the Prophets
5. Sermon
6. Psalm selections (congregational responses)
7. Benediction ("amen" response)

As a rabbi visiting the Nazareth synagogue, Christ read from the prophetic section of Isaiah 61. He may have been given the opportunity to choose which passage he read, or perhaps this passage was a lectionary selection that was assigned to him—the Torah was divided into weekly sections, and in the synagogues it was customarily read through in its entirety over a three-year cycle. Whether this text was chosen by Jesus or assigned to him, it pointed directly to him. The purpose of Scripture is always to point us to Christ, the living Word.[4]

---

4. Scripture's Christ-centered focus is seen when Christ himself meets on Easter Sunday with Cleopas and his companion: "And beginning with Moses and all the Prophets, he explained to them what was said in all the Scriptures concerning himself" (Luke 24:27). Later, he says to all his assembled disciples, "Everything must be fulfilled that is written about me in the Law of Moses, the Prophets and the Psalms" (v. 44).

Standing to Read Scripture

Luke 4:16 says that Jesus "stood up to read." In synagogue worship, the reader would stand to present Scripture and then sit for the preaching part of the service.[5] Standing to read conveys an attitude of attentive respect for Scripture. We might draw the implication from this ancient practice that the reading of Scripture in our services today should be viewed as essential and be received with reverent respect.

Expositing Scripture

In every synagogue service, an exposition of Scripture followed the reading of it. This sermon was delivered by a preacher who sat on a chair or throne on an elevated platform. Luke doesn't record Christ's entire sermon in Nazareth, but he succinctly summarizes it with the words "Today this scripture is fulfilled in your hearing" (4:21).

Let's Apply This

The worship service of the synagogue is the precursor of those in today's churches. A form of the word *synagogue* is employed in Hebrews 10:25, which tells us that we should be "not giving up *meeting together* [*episunagogen*], as some are in the habit of doing, but encouraging one another—and all the more as you see the Day approaching." When you and I gather for worship on Sundays, we follow a pattern that had its early beginnings in the tabernacle, moved to the temple, and then transitioned to the synagogue. The model of worship that Christ gave us in the synagogue in Nazareth teaches us that Scripture should be conspicuously present in our worship services. Liturgies should be soaked in Scripture.

---

5. We do have an example in Acts 13:16 of Paul standing while he taught in the synagogue, which perhaps reflects a different practice in the Diaspora areas.

The apostle Paul was very conscious of this when he passed on these pieces of inspired counsel to the young church leader Timothy: "Devote yourself to the public reading of Scripture, to preaching and to teaching" (1 Tim. 4:13); "Preach the Word" (2 Tim. 4:2).

Christians, as well as the Jewish people, have often been called "people of the book." From the very beginning, the reading and teaching of Scripture has been at the heart of Christian worship. Nowadays, we take for granted that television, video screens, computer monitors, tablets, smartphones, and video games will vie for our attention—not only at work but also in the grocery store, in the coffee shop, at the gas station pump, in sports bars, and in many other weekday locations. But, come Sunday, we step into another world—a church sanctuary in which often just one person stands in order to read and preach from an ancient book for twenty-five to fifty minutes, with no visual images in sight. The central article of furniture in the room is usually a pulpit or a clear Plexiglas stand, on which rests a book—hopefully a Bible.

So what implications does this shift from words to images in our society, which is so much a part of our lives outside the church, have for our worship services? Certainly that's a question that merits reflection and perhaps discussion. How does your church measure up to the "word-centeredness" of the early synagogue? Do changes need to be made? Should we not be concerned when Scripture readings are squeezed out of services because there isn't time for them, or when the preaching of the Word is truncated into a quick several-minute homily or replaced with another, more relevant activity?

There is more that could be said about the history of synagogues and their influence on how the church was shaped and about the possible parallels between synagogue worship and our worship practices today. But it's time to return to the mountains in order to discover further dimensions of worship. In the next chapter we'll continue the story by traveling to yet another mountain.

Questions for Reflection and Discussion

1. Have you ever attended a modern synagogue service? If so, describe your experience.
2. What do some scholars suggest was the origin of synagogues?
3. How do you think the shift from a word-centered to an image-centered culture has impacted and will continue to impact corporate worship services? Can or should we resist this?
4. "Should we not be concerned when Scripture readings are squeezed out of services because there isn't time for them, or when the preaching of the Word is truncated into a quick several-minute homily or replaced with another, more relevant activity?" Have you seen any examples of this?
5. What are some ways that the synagogue service in Nazareth demonstrated the centrality of Scripture in worship?
6. What are the direct and indirect ways in which Scripture is present in and influences the worship that occurs in your church?
7. What are some ways that you could personally elevate the importance of Scripture when you attend worship services?

9

LIFTING THE VEIL

Mount Hermon: Mountain of Transfigured Worship

Worship is the right, fitting, and delightful response of moral
beings—angelic and human—to God the Creator, Redeemer,
and Consummator, for who he is as one eternal God in three
persons—Father, Son, and Holy Spirit—and for what he
has done in creation and redemption, and for what he will
do in the coming consummation, to whom be all praise
and glory, now and forever, world without end. Amen.
—Jonathan Gibson, in *Reformation Worship*

When I was an undergraduate student at a liberal arts college in
New York, I was encouraged to subscribe to a weekly news magazine—either *Newsweek* or *Time*. I chose the latter. That set me
on a path that I've continued to follow. I try to read *Time* with
discernment, using the filter of a biblical world- and life-view.
I still find that the weekly magazine is informative and that it helps
me to understand the pulse of today's changing culture.

One of the annual issues of *Time* that I look forward to reading contains the cover story on the one hundred most influential

people in the world. It's an extended article that fosters worship—in this case, the worship of human celebrities! The editors single out public figures from the worlds of politics, business, entertainment, education, sports, and technology, as well as from other fields. These anointed celebrities include the likes of Tim Cook, Jeff Bezos, Xi Jinping, Kim Kardashian, Lady Gaga, Vladimir Putin, Pope Francis, and of course the K-pop group BTS. The list proves to be a revolving parade of influencers who are singled out one year but long forgotten by the next year. New celebrity figures continue to walk onto the world's restless stage and grab our attention. But year after year the editors fail to recognize the one living person who deserves to be honored above every other individual on their list.

By all comparisons, the living, resurrected Jesus of Nazareth should stand out as the most influential and significant person who was ever born on this planet—ranking above Confucius, Buddha, Muhammad, and every other prophet, president, and ruler on earth. He alone is worthy of our total worship, because he appeared on earth in incarnate form as the unique Son of God and brought to fulfillment all the Old Testament types and shadows that we have discussed in previous chapters. Jesus alone should be our central focus when we assemble for worship celebrations at the beginning of each week.

In this chapter, we will turn our attention to the story of the transfiguration of Jesus. The narrative is important enough to be repeated in all three Synoptic Gospels, although we'll limit our focus mainly to the account reported by Luke the physician in 9:27–36. As we look at this story, let me remind you that we are dealing not with mythology or creative fiction but rather with an actual historical event. Dr. Luke's meticulous attention to detail gives his readers a front-row seat to watch the circumstances leading up to the transfiguration of Christ on an unnamed mountain in Israel.

A Surprising Prediction

In Luke 9:27–28 we read these words:

"Truly I tell you, some who are standing here will not taste death before they see the kingdom of God."

About eight days after Jesus said this, he took Peter, John and James with him and went up onto a mountain to pray.

Just prior to this prediction, Peter had made his famous public confession of belief in Jesus as the Messiah. Soon after, Jesus began to warn his disciples of his impending death and resurrection. The reality of what was going to happen probably did not sink in with them—at least not all the way. No doubt the disciples were baffled even further when Jesus told them that some of them would actually see the kingdom of God before they themselves died. Exactly what was this kingdom they were going to see? What was Jesus predicting?

First-century Jews had an optimistic expectation that when the Messiah appeared he would gather a large following, address the corruption in Jerusalem, and overthrow the oppressive rule of the occupying Roman government. Many Jews anticipated a physical, earthly kingdom that would restore Israel to its former glory. But this was a misguided expectation. Jesus predicted a different path for the kingdom that he was bringing and over which he would reign.

In this context, Jesus singled out three of his disciples to receive a foretaste of the kingdom to come. What was about to unfold before their eyes was a behind-the-scenes glimpse, an unexpected unveiling, of the heavenly agenda that Jesus had planned for his followers.

Throughout Luke's gospel, Jesus is often described spending extended periods of time in prayer when he faced critical

decisions or anticipated significant turning points in his ministry. This was one of those times. Jesus knew that he needed to
escape the crowds in order to spend time with his Father. And so
he retreated to a mountain. The text doesn't name the mountain,
but the parallel gospel accounts reported by Matthew and Mark
both call it a "high mountain."

Which Mountain Did He Choose?

In traditional teaching, the mountain of transfiguration is
Mount Tabor—a dome-shaped elevation, like an upside-down
teacup, that rises out of the fairly flat Jezreel Valley. It's southwest
of the Sea of Galilee and only about four and a half miles from
Nazareth. Tourists find it to be an easily recognizable summit.
As early as the third century, the Greek scholar and theologian
Origen conjectured that Tabor was the likely location of the
Mount of Transfiguration. My wife and I chose not to climb the
4,340 steps to the top of this summit. Instead, we drove up the
narrow, winding road of hairpin curves and cliffs that overlooks
the Valley of Armageddon below.

With all due respect to traditionalists, I find myself in the
growing ranks of those who believe that a more likely candidate
for the site of the transfiguration is Mount Hermon, near the
adjoining borders of Israel, Syria, and Lebanon. It is part of the
southern end of the Anti-Lebanon mountain range, and all three
bordering countries claim rights to a portion of Mount Hermon.
During early Canaanite history it was regarded as a sacred site,
and a temple to Baal was erected on it. Various other ancient
temples have been found in villages on its slopes. The summit is
located about twenty-five miles north of the Sea of Galilee. On
a clear day it can be seen even from the Dead Sea, which is over
a hundred miles to the south. At 9,262 feet in elevation, Mount
Hermon is approximately four times the height of Mount Tabor.

This altitude explains why the mountain is often snow-covered for two-thirds of the year and why it happens to be the proud host of Israel's only ski resort. Locals call it Snowy Mountain and the Gray-Haired Mountain. Since both Matthew and Mark tell us that the site of the transfiguration was a "high mountain," Hermon, being the highest summit in Israel, seems to fit the bill more readily than the far smaller Mount Tabor does.

In the days leading up to this event, Jesus had spent time in the villages around Caesarea Philippi, which is a mere seven miles south of the slopes of Mount Hermon. For this reason also, it seems likely that this nearby mountain that was the highest in Israel was the location where Jesus climbed—along with Peter, James, and John, his three students-in-training—to spend time in solitude and prayer as the end of his earthly ministry approached.

Significance of This Mountaintop Experience with Christ

By now you've caught on to the fact that I have a special love for mountains. But I'll readily admit that the mountain event that Luke describes here has no parallels in my travels. This was a one-time, totally unique event. On this mountain, the veil was pulled away from the hidden God, and in the process the disciples witnessed visual phenomena and heard an auditory voice that surely must have remained in their memory for the rest of their lives.[1] They had climbed the mountain in order to pray with Jesus, but nothing could have prepared them for what they were about to experience.

As we delve into this narrative, may it compel us to worship.

---

1. Some years after the transfiguration, Peter referred, in 2 Peter 1:17–18, to the memory of being "with him on the sacred mountain."

Metamorphosis

First, the disciples noticed a change in Jesus's face, as it took on an otherworldly glow (see Luke 9:29). The parallel accounts in Matthew and Mark use the Greek term *metamorphoo* to describe this change. This is the Greek word from which we get the English word "metamorphosis." On this occasion, Christ's outward facial appearance was being changed—but not because an external light was shining on him. Rather, his divine internal glory was shining outward. The disciples may have been tempted at first to think that they were hallucinating.

Something similar happened to Moses when he descended Mount Sinai after receiving the Decalogue. Exodus 34:29 explains, "When Moses came down from Mount Sinai with the two tablets of the covenant law in his hands, he was not aware that his face was radiant because he had spoken with the LORD." The radiance on the face of Moses, however, was different. It was an external reflection of God's glory, not an internal reflection of his own glory.

Now, hundreds of years later, as he is praying on another mountain, Jesus's appearance is remarkably changed before the eyes of the watching disciples. His entire body is suddenly bathed in heavenly light. Mark tells us that "his clothes became dazzling white, whiter than anyone in the world could bleach them" (9:3), and Luke records that "his clothes became as bright as a flash of lightning" (9:29). Throughout the Bible, light is often used as a sign of God's holy presence.

Visitors from Another Dimension

The disciples have every reason to be reeling over what they have just witnessed—but even more is about to happen! They now catch sight of two other men on the mountain who seem to be in deep conversation with Jesus. Peter, James, and John immediately recognize these men to be the Old Testament heroes Moses and Elijah. Can you imagine how startled these three young Jewish disciples must have been? After all, Moses had died more than 1,480 years earlier, and no one knew where he had been buried. Elijah had exited this earth about nine hundred years before the transfiguration and had been taken up by God into the sky in a whirlwind. Yet these prominent Old Testament figures were now alive and talking with Jesus! The hidden God was unveiling for these select disciples what had previously been to them an invisible dimension.

What does Scripture tell us about the conversation that took place in this holy huddle? "They spoke about his departure, which he was about to bring to fulfillment at Jerusalem" (Luke 9:31). The term that is translated into English as "departure" is the Greek word *exodus*. Jesus was about to head southward from the mountain to the city of Jerusalem, where he would be crucified and resurrected before ascending back to the Father in the heavenly dimension. His time of exodus from earth was nearing. It is likely that Moses and Elijah came to encourage, affirm, and perhaps celebrate Christ's agenda for completing his redemptive work. They had long anticipated this agenda. The transfiguration that the disciples witnessed that day on the mountain anticipated another supernatural event that would soon occur on another mountain (which we will climb in the next chapter)—Christ's ascension from the Mount of Olives.

Because the transfiguration is a familiar story for many Christians, it is easy to skim over the narrative. So let me raise this question: why, out of all the people in the Old Testament, were Moses and Elijah singled out to make this trip to Mount Hermon? Could it be because of what each of them represented in Old Testament history?

Moses represented the law. He had been part of God's plan to deliver his people from slavery and bondage in Egypt. He had led the exodus out of Egypt. Now Christ was about to experience another kind of extraordinary exodus. As Moses's counterpart,

Elijah represented the prophets. Like Moses, he had been part of God's plan to deliver his people from bondage. In Elijah's case, this was bondage to the Canaanite deity Baal.

The two key figures from Mount Sinai and Mount Carmel now stood on Mount Hermon with the One to whom their ministries had pointed. What Christ was about to accomplish would bring to completion what Moses and Elijah had anticipated.

A Glory Cloud

The disciples experienced yet another layer of transcendence with Jesus on the mountain: "A cloud appeared and covered them, and they were afraid as they entered the cloud" (Luke 9:34).

If you have tracked the biblical story of worship with us from the beginning of this book, it should be obvious what's happening here. At Mount Sinai, a cloud had appeared as God descended on the mountain and met with Moses. At the dedication of the tabernacle, a cloud had descended that the Israelites recognized as a symbol of the presence of God. At the dedication of the temple, the same cloud had appeared and descended, indicating that God was in their midst. Now, on the Mount of Transfiguration, the cloud appeared again. This time it enveloped Jesus and the others who were with him on the mountain. When the cloud lifted, Moses and Elijah had disappeared.

Peter, James, and John were young Jewish men who had likely grown up hearing the Old Testament stories about the *kabod* glory cloud. They would have recognized immediately that a cloud like this could mean only one thing. Imagine the impact that this event had on Peter, who not long before this had passionately confessed his belief in Jesus as the unique Son of God!

In the disciples' minds, the visual phenomena that accompanied the transfiguration were a powerful confirmation that Jesus was who he claimed to be: the incarnate Son of God. All the visual signs pointed to Jesus as being uniquely worthy of worship.

Fig. 9.1. Further Recurrence of the Glory Cloud

Auditory Voice

The disciples must have been even more startled to hear the Father's voice address them: "This is my Son, whom I have chosen; listen to him" (Luke 9:35). This divine statement, as it reverberated off the mountain, confirmed still more explicitly that the person whom the disciples were following was the unique Son of God. This was an experience that would put steel in their spines to prepare them for the difficult days of testing that were rapidly approaching.

Christ knew what lay ahead for his disciples. He knew that they were on course to become leaders of the early church. Under their leadership, the church would gather each Lord's Day to worship the resurrected Christ. The transfiguration event that they had witnessed proved to the disciples that Christ was worthy of being followed and worshipped for the rest of their lives. For a brief period of time, the veil that separated the heavenly dimension from their world had been lifted. God had staged the event for a purpose.

Applying the Mountaintop Event to Our Lives

Lest we leave this story as just a fascinating piece of dusty history, let's look at how Christ's transfiguration on the mountain should fuel our own worship. There is much more to worship than sentimentality about Jesus. True worship is rooted in the person and work of Christ. The full scope of his identity and mission provides the theological foundation for Christ-centered worship. So what does this event teach us about why we should be motivated to worship the transfigured Christ?

Christ Is Divine

The transfiguration was a powerful affirmation of Christ's divine, transcendent identity. In the weeks prior to the transfiguration, people had been asking who this itinerant teacher was, who traveled from town to town teaching and working miracles. At Caesarea Philippi, Jesus directly asked his disciples who they believed he was. This question prompted Peter to make his dramatic, definitive declaration that Jesus was the divine Messiah. The encounter on the Mount of Transfiguration should have clinched Christ's identity for the disciples who were present. How could they not believe?

I appreciate how one commentator applies this story to today's world: "The heavenly voice notes that [Jesus] transcends all cultures and is called to minister to all humanity as God's chosen servant. He is the ultimate multicultural figure, calling everyone to himself in the ultimate equal opportunity call. The world does not need the clash of competing religious figures and examples. It needs a Savior for all humanity. The Transfiguration is a divine declaration that such a unique figure exists, and the world should listen to him."[2]

In Christ, Death Loses Its Power

It had been 1,480 years since Moses's mysterious death and more than nine hundred years since Elijah had been raptured

---

2. Darrell L. Bock, *Luke*, The NIV Application Commentary (Grand Rapids: Zondervan, 1996), 273.

and taken to heaven. Nevertheless, both Old Testament figures appeared with Christ on the mountain. In Christ's kingdom, death has lost its power. Moses and Elijah hadn't dissolved into ashes that were scattered on the Sea of Galilee, never to appear again as persons. When the supernatural veil was lifted, Moses and Elijah were very much alive and able to converse with Christ. That's a picture of the reality of the heavenly kingdom. In the future new heaven and new earth, there will be no need for a barrier between the living and the dead. All believers will enjoy the immediate presence of God. We can be confident that death will not end our existence. This story is a stunning proof of the afterlife.

Like Christ, We Will Be Transformed

This mountaintop scene gives us a glimpse into the perfect kingdom that Christ's death, resurrection, and ascension will bring to pass for us. We have every hope for the future. The comforting promises in Romans 8 make that clear:

> I consider that our present sufferings are not worth comparing with the glory that will be revealed in us. . . .
>
> We know that the whole creation has been groaning as in the pains of childbirth right up to the present time. Not only so, but we ourselves, who have the firstfruits of the Spirit, groan inwardly as we wait eagerly for our adoption to sonship, the redemption of our bodies. For in this hope we were saved. (vv. 18, 22–24)

Christ knew that the road ahead of him included his arrest in the garden, an unjust trial, false accusations, scourging by soldiers, mocking by the crowd of onlookers, nails being driven into his hands and feet, a spear being pierced into his side, and slow death on a shameful cross. The agony of the cross was beyond description, but it had to be endured in order for Christ to experience the glory of the resurrection, the ascension, and the exaltation at the right hand of the Father in heaven.

Bible teacher Chuck Swindoll has reminded us,

> We can have confidence—despite the many challenges to our faith—that pursuing God's plan is always best, even if it leads through suffering, pain, and all the way to death. While we endure the dominion of evil now, a glorious future awaits the faithful. Some pay a huge price for their decision to follow Christ. Some lose contact with their families, some endure social and cultural rejection, some even risk losing their lives for the sake of trusting in Christ. Others may not face difficulties as extreme, but the decision to become a follower of Jesus Christ opens the believer to spiritual attacks. On top of those difficulties, life can be hard. In fact, sometimes the decision to forsake Christ can appear easier. The transfiguration is our reminder today: stay with God's plan! There is none better—even if it means suffering and pain, all the way to death. Stay the course. The glory of God awaits you at the end of your journey.[3]

In the future kingdom, our bodies will not be impacted by pain, suffering, thirst, hunger, disease, or anything evil. Imagine a world with no more need for shelter, medicine, hospitals, armies, guns, metal detectors, computer virus protection, or counterterrorism.

Looking to Jesus: Two Stories

A young theologian and father of two young children received a gut-wrenching diagnosis of a rare form of cancer that had no known treatment. He wrote a poignant article about his need to

---

3. Charles R. Swindoll, *Insights on Luke*, Swindoll's New Testament Insights (Grand Rapids: Zondervan, 2012), 241.

keep his eyes focused on Jesus no matter what. "His ways remain hidden to those without faith, but those with faith see the glory of God revealed in the face of Jesus Christ. When you see Jesus, you see the invisible God made visible. So look to Jesus."[4]

How do you and I stay the course and remain faithful to the end? There is only one way—by keeping our eyes on the One who was transfigured on the mountain. The Father's instruction to the disciples was "Listen to him." The experience on the Mountain of Transfiguration was an unrepeatable event. We cannot return to it—but we can return again and again to the written Word. And what does that Word remind us? "We all, who with unveiled faces contemplate the Lord's glory, are being transformed into his image with ever-increasing glory, which comes from the Lord, who is the Spirit" (2 Cor. 3:18).

A woman named Helen Howarth Lemmel (1863–1961) emigrated with her family from England to the United States when she was only twelve years old. She is remembered as an extraordinarily gifted vocalist and the prolific composer of many beloved hymns and choruses. Her story is difficult to verify, but many sources report that she was troubled throughout her life with serious health issues and eventually became totally blind. One of the nearly five hundred hymns that Helen wrote, "The Heavenly Vison," became a well-known and beloved song. It is more widely known as "Turn Your Eyes upon Jesus."[5]

O soul are you weary and troubled?
No light in the darkness you see?

4. Bobby Grow, "God Behind the Veil," *Christianity Today*, April 1, 2013, https://www.christianitytoday.com/ct/2013/may/god-behind-veil.html.
5. If you subscribe to an online music service, perhaps you could locate and play for yourself or your study group one of the many versions of this hymn. Written in 1922, the hymn is now in public domain and can be easily found on the internet.

There's light for a look at the Savior,
And life more abundant and free!
Turn your eyes upon Jesus.
Look full in his wonderful face.
And the things of earth will grow strangely dim
In the light of his glory and grace.

The next time you enter a worship assembly, remember this invitation as you focus your attention on the transfigured Christ.

Questions for Reflection and Discussion

1. Bible scholars differ on which mountain they identify as the actual Mount of Transfiguration. Which mountain do you think it was, and why?
2. What are the similarities and differences between Moses's experience on Mount Sinai and Christ's experience on the Mount of Transfiguration?
3. What is the significance of Moses and Elijah's appearing on the mountain with Christ? What other mountains are these men associated with?
4. Read through Luke 9:27–36 and discuss reasons why Christ is worthy of our worship.
5. What does this account in Luke reveal about life after death?
6. What do you find in the story of Helen Lemmel that can bring direction and encouragement?
7. The story of the transfiguration is important enough to be included in all three Synoptic Gospels. Why is it important, and what would we miss if it had not been included in Scripture?

10

DISAPPEARANCE
WITH A PURPOSE

Mount of Olives: Mountain
of Ascended Worship

*In the Old Testament, we find instances where God comes
by descending in a cloud. Here, God, in the person of Jesus,
ascends. In Old Testament theophanies, God appears in a cloud.
Here, he disappears in a cloud. In Ezekiel 1, the theophany
progressively reveals to Ezekiel a cloud, living creatures, and
then a human figure in the center. Here, Jesus is the human
figure in the center, but the movement of events and of textual
focus goes from Jesus to the cloud, and finally to angelic figures.*
—Vern S. Poythress, *Theophany*

A recent issue of Wheaton College's alumni magazine arrived in
my mailbox and received more than my usual cursory glance and
toss into the recycling bin. One article in particular grabbed my
attention. It described various revivals that have broken out and
spread like wildfire on the campus of Wheaton College since its
founding—perhaps ten revivals prior to 1900, and then again in

1936, 1943, 1950, 1970, and 1995. All these revivals were special visitations of God's presence. One Wheaton student testified, "I was especially blessed by the presence of God and felt an unusual sense of joy in worship." He went on to explain that "I have never felt that kind of presence of God before. I was overwhelmed to the point of laughing and crying at the same time in the presence of the Lord as we worshipped Him that Thursday night." Another student described God's presence as being "just so strong and so thick."[1] Does that stir a sense of longing in your own soul? Do you want to experience that kind of reality?

I realized anew the importance of what these students had expressed when I read these words from John J. Davis: "If enjoying God and being in the presence of God is the highest purpose for which I exist, then worship and biblical meditation are not low priorities but high priorities; they are worthy of my best time, energy and focused attention."[2] I highlighted these words and nodded my head in wholehearted agreement. To be honest, this is what has motivated me to teach on the subject of biblical worship for many years. It is also what is motivating me to write this book. This God-centered reality is what the students at Wheaton experienced during those visitations.

How do we explain their experience? No one has claimed that a physical, bodily encounter with the ascended Christ ever happened on Wheaton's campus or on any other college campus. Revivals, wherever they may occur, are only one among many ways in which God may choose to manifest his presence in the post-incarnation and post-ascension era in which we live. In the pages to follow, we will look at some of them.

---

1. Rich McLaughlin, "The Essence of Revival," *Wheaton* 18, no. 2 (Spring 2015), 19.

2. John Jefferson Davis, *Meditation and Communion with God: Contemplating Scripture in an Age of Distraction* (Downers Grove, IL: IVP Academic, 2012), 87.

Understanding God's Presence

Before we climb the next mountain, let's briefly summarize some key concepts about the presence of God.

Fig. 10.1. Umbrella: God's Plan to Restore His Unmediated Presence

We have seen so far that the dominant reality of worship is the presence of God. It can be pictured as an overarching umbrella that begins in the garden of Eden in Genesis and culminates in the fulfilled and restored garden city or heavenly city in Revelation. Genesis 1–3 finds a mirrored fulfillment in Revelation 21–22. These opening and closing chapters have been pictured as the bookends of the Bible.

Anyone who has ever attempted to find words to describe God's presence knows how difficult it is to capture the ancient mystery of the one whom some call *mysterium tremendum*. Although risks and dangers exist when we try to explain this mystery, the following chart attempts to succinctly point out the several forms that God's presence takes in the past, present, and future:

Seven Dimensions of Presence	Scripture References	Capsule Summary
God's omnipresence filling every square inch of the universe eternally.	"Where can I go from your Spirit? Where can I flee from your presence?" (Ps. 139:7).	Christ everywhere
Old Testament manifestations of God's presence at altars and in the cloud at Sinai, the tabernacle, and the temple.	"I am going to come to you in a dense cloud" (Ex. 19:9). "So the cloud of the LORD was over the tabernacle by day, and fire was in the cloud by night, in the sight of all the Israelites during all their travels" (Ex. 40:38). "Then the temple of the LORD was filled with the cloud" (2 Chron. 5:13).	Christ in special places
Christ being physically, temporally present in the incarnation.	"The Word became flesh and made his dwelling among us" (John 1:14).	Christ on earth

Christ sitting at the right hand of the Father's throne, from his ascension to the present.	"He sat down at the right hand of the Majesty in heaven" (Heb. 1:3).	Christ above us
God's Spirit indwelling believers from after his ascension to the present.	"Christ in you, the hope of glory" (Col. 1:27).	Christ within us
Christ being spiritually present in worship assemblies and at the Lord's table.	"When you are assembled . . . and the power of our Lord Jesus is present" (1 Cor. 5:4).	Christ among us
God's direct, eternal presence in the new heaven and earth.	"God's dwelling place is now among the people, and he will dwell with them. They will be his people, and God himself will be with them and be their God" (Rev. 21:3).	Christ with us

Against this background and context, let's consider another mountain event that has powerful implications for our experience of worship each Sunday. God's drawing near to a summit comes at a pivotal transition, as we move to the sixth mountain that we are visiting in this book.

The Context of the Mount of Olives
Ascension Event Following the Crucifixion[3]

In the last chapter we saw that Christ's mountaintop transfiguration marked the beginning of his journey to Jerusalem, where he would face his atoning death, which marked the end of the Old Testament sacrificial system in the temple. Christ's crucifixion continues to leave its mark in the redemptive focus of our worship today. Let's now trace the unfolding story of redemption onward from the cross and the empty tomb to the mountaintop event that we will examine in this chapter.

The timing of the ascension of Jesus is not hard to pinpoint. Scripture tells us that it occurred forty days after the first Easter, when Christ experienced a bodily resurrection, and ten days before the feast of Pentecost, when the third person of the Trinity came to indwell believers. Luke refers to this forty-day period in the opening chapter of his Acts account: "[Jesus] appeared to them over a period of forty days and spoke about the kingdom of God" (v. 3). If you count forward forty days from Easter Sunday, you realize that the departure of Christ from earth took place on a Thursday, not on a Sunday. Perhaps this explains why Ascension Day so easily slips past us unnoticed.

What do we know about the location of the ascension event? The New Testament places a pin on the map in the vicinity of Bethany—the town that Luke identifies in his gospel (see 24:50). Yet Luke later identifies the location as "the mount called Olivet, which is near Jerusalem" (Acts 1:12 ESV).

---

3. Some readers may have wondered why Golgotha, the site of Christ's crucifixion, was not included as a mountain of worship in a separate chapter. All four gospel accounts of the crucifixion fail to identify Golgotha as a mountain or even a hill. Some people have speculated that it may have been a small raised ridge. The idea in the minds of some Christians that it was a hill or mountain may come from the extrabiblical hymn lyrics "On a hill far away stood an old rugged cross." While

As it turns out, it is not at all difficult to reconcile these two locations. Both are accurate, because Bethany was a village that was located on the southern slopes of the Mount of Olives. The mountain itself was a rounded ridge that had four identifiable summits. It was named for the olive groves that covered much of its surface in biblical times. The site is composed of cretaceous limestone and forms the highest range of hills east of Jerusalem, at 2,600 feet above sea level. This places its summit at an elevation that is 250 feet higher than the nearby Temple Mount.

Travelers who visit the Mount of Olives today are able to take in a sweeping view of the city of Jerusalem to the west. The panorama is especially glorious in the early morning, before the hordes of tourists arrive, when the rising sun lights up the golden Dome of the Rock and surroundings. It is easy to understand why the Romans sometimes called the northern extension of the ridge "The Lookout" or "Mount Scopus." Josephus refers to this location "from whence the city began already to be seen, and a plain view might be taken of the great temple." He goes on to refer to this mount, "which lies over against the city on the east side, and is parted from it by a deep valley, interposed between them, which is named Cedron."[4] Today we call this the Kidron Valley; it separates the Mount of Olives and the city of Jerusalem.

This mountain had a rich history that dated back to Old Testament times. Sadly, the famous King Solomon, who erected the glorious temple on Mount Zion on the opposite side of the Kidron valley, built on this summit altars to Chemosh, the detestable god of Moab, and to Molek the god of the Ammonites to whom children were sacrificed (see 1 Kings 11:7). Many centuries

---

the crucifixion was highly significant for our worship, it doesn't fit into the category of a public assembly of worship on an identifiable mountain.

4. Josephus, *The Wars of the Jews*, bk. 5, chap. 2.3, in *The Works of Josephus: Complete and Unabridged*, new updated ed., trans. William Whiston (Peabody, MA: Hendrickson Publishers, 1987).

later, these pagan idols and altars on the Mount of Olives were destroyed by Judah's last good ruler, King Josiah (ca. 640–609 BC)—the sixteenth king to follow Solomon. When Josiah assumed office, Judah had already sunk to its lowest. Immorality and idolatry were pervasive. During Josiah's reign, an era of spiritual reform began, idol worship was abolished, and worship of the true God was reinstated.

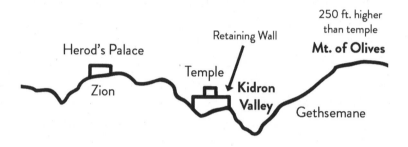

Fig. 10.2. Location of Christ's Ascension

A New Era of Redemptive History

The significance of Christ's incarnation was deeply embedded into my thinking from my early childhood—especially at Christmastime. Our family lived in the parsonage next door to the church where my dad was the pastor. My parents believed it would be a witness to our neighbors and would spread Christmas cheer in the neighborhood if we played Christmas carols on an outdoor amplified speaker. My second-floor bedroom, and the flat porch roof that extended from it, was the chosen location for the dubious sound equipment. To this day, I have the most delightful memories of falling asleep to the music that wafted into the frigid winter air outside my bedroom window. Passersby would hear the music and sometimes sing along to familiar words from one of my favorite carols:

Christ, by highest Heav'n adored; Christ the everlasting Lord;
Late in time, behold Him come, offspring of a virgin's womb.
Veiled in flesh the Godhead see; hail th'incarnate Deity,
Pleased as man with man to dwell, Jesus our Immanuel.[5]

Night after night, the joyful message of good news echoed through the streets of our little hamlet in western New York. Yes, God did come to dwell on earth. The God who was present with Adam and Eve in the garden, who after their fall into sin promised to send a Redeemer, did indeed keep his promise. The incarnate Savior who appeared on earth in first-century Bethlehem as Immanuel was the long-awaited fulfillment of that promise. Christ's earthly ministry culminated in his redemptive sacrifice on Golgotha. His resurrection validated his deity and marked the completion of his earthly ministry. A new era of redemptive history began when Christ returned to his Father in heaven.

Reasons for This Location

Out of all the places from which Jesus could have made his earthly exodus, why this mountain on the eastern edge of Jerusalem? Why the Mount of Olives? Several possible reasons have been suggested.

Proximity to Jerusalem

Among other reasons, Jesus may have chosen the Mount of Olives because of its easy access to Jerusalem—it was only "a Sabbath day's journey away" (Acts 1:12 ESV). The Jewish Mishnah tells us that travel on the Sabbath was limited to a distance of 2000 cubits.[6] That would be equivalent to between half

5. Charles Wesley, "Hark! The Herald Angels Sing," 1739.
6. See Sotah 5:3.

and two-thirds of a mile—much less than the ten thousand steps of exercise (almost five miles' worth) that some of us aim to clock each day. Since the Mount of Olives was less than a mile from the city of Jerusalem, access to the summit was convenient, quick, and easy.

Favored Location

The Mount of Olives had often been a favorite place for Jesus to visit. In the first century, the shaded slopes of the mountain made it a desirable place to find relief from the bustle of city streets. While the population of Jerusalem was much smaller in the first century than it is today, people enjoyed retreating to this quiet, shady spot away from the commotion of commerce. Luke mentions that Jesus regularly frequented this location. "He came out and went, as was his custom, to the Mount of Olives" (22:39 ESV). So it seems natural that Jesus would come to this familiar place, away from the gawking crowds, for his ascension back to heaven.

Symbolic Significance

Jesus may also have selected this location for its symbolic significance. This was the place where the enthusiastic crowds had waved palm branches and descended into Jerusalem in procession on the Sunday before the crucifixion (see Matt. 21:1; Mark 11:1). Now that the cross event was accomplished, Jesus's triumphant entrance into the earthly Jerusalem would be matched by a triumphant exit to the heavenly Jerusalem.

Personal Significance

The garden of Gethsemane—the place where Jesus had prayed in willing submission to the Father on the night of his betrayal just a few weeks beforehand—was located on the lower slopes of the Mount of Olives.

A few years ago, after a long day of walking the streets of Jerusalem, I was overcome with a longing to spend time in the garden of Gethsemane area under the cover of darkness, as Jesus had done. I exited through the Lion's Gate of the Old City and headed in that direction on foot. No one knows for sure the exact location of the garden of Gethsemane, but the traditional site is the area on which the Roman Catholic Church of All Nations now stands. Outside that church is a garden of ancient olive trees with gnarled trunks. Carbon dating of the oldest trees in that garden reveal that the trees likely date back to the twelfth century AD. Some scientists believe that these present olive trees may have grown from the root systems of trees that were standing over two thousand years ago, when Christ spent time in the garden.

Despite uncertainty about the precise location of the garden of Gethsemane, just being in the general area where Christ had agonized in prayer prior to his arrest evoked within me deep emotion and a sense of overwhelming unworthiness and gratitude. Reflecting that night on the events that led up to the crucifixion, I realized how easily Christ could have bolted from the garden and disappeared into the nearby wilderness under the cover of darkness. Instead he cried from the depths of his soul, "May your will be done." God's sovereign plan would not be thwarted.

Prophetic Significance

An enigmatic prophecy of Zechariah seems to suggest that the visible, physical return of Christ will be on the Mount of Olives. Zechariah prophesied, "On that day his feet shall stand on the Mount of Olives that lies before Jerusalem on the east, and the Mount of Olives shall be split in two from east to west by a very wide valley, so that one half of the Mount shall move northward, and the other half southward" (14:4). According to tradition, the prophet Zechariah is buried on the Mount of Olives, amid over

150,000 graves and tombs—some of which date back over three thousand years.

Eyewitness Reports

Fortunately for us, the events surrounding Christ's ascension are well documented and corroborated. Dr. Luke tells us that he carefully interviewed eyewitnesses, and later, under the Spirit's inspiration, he recorded their narrative in the last chapter of his gospel and the first chapter of the book of Acts. From these Spirit-inspired passages, we can piece together the succession of events.

Luke records that Jesus lifted his hands and blessed the disciples who surrounded him. Subsequently, he was parted from the disciples and carried up into heaven. As he supernaturally ascended out of the earthly dimension, he was surrounded by a cloud. This was no ordinary nimbus, stratus, or cumulous cloud that just happened to be drifting in from the Mediterranean coast. Rather, it appears to be the heavy cloud of glory, the *kabod* cloud, which had been visible at the Old Testament tabernacle and temple and had enveloped Christ on the Mount of Transfiguration. Once again it announced the divine presence and confirmed that the One who was ascending was not just one among many young Jewish rabbis but uniquely God's Son—deity in human form.

We can't possibly imagine the thoughts and raw emotions that the watching disciples experienced. Did they understand that what they had just witnessed represented the continuation, not the cessation, of Christ's work as Lord and Messiah? Luke records that as the disciples continued to gaze upward at their departing Redeemer, angelic beings appeared to them and announced the comforting promise of Christ's visible return. "This Jesus, who was taken up from you into heaven, will come in the same way as you saw him go into heaven" (Acts 1:11 ESV). In other words, his anticipated future return would mirror his departure into heaven that they had seen.

It should not surprise us that the disciples' immediate response to what they had witnessed and to the angels' promise was to worship their ascended Lord.

> And they worshiped him and returned to Jerusalem with great joy, and were continually in the temple blessing God. (Luke 24:52–53 ESV)

These verses assure us that the disciples did not leave the scene of the ascension heartbroken. Following the angels' announcement, they returned to Jerusalem energized to worship the Christ who had returned to his former glory and would one day come again.

The Theological Meaning of This Mountain Event

The ascension holds unique theological significance for Christ as well as for us. Let's begin by looking at several things that the ascension meant for Christ.

His Redemptive Work Was Complete

On his ascension to heaven, Christ took his seat at the right hand of the Father—what theologians call the "session" of Christ. Through him, the Old Testament forms, ceremonies, types, and shadows of worship that were seen in the tabernacle, temple, and sacrificial system had been brought to fulfillment. As the apostle Paul explains, "He [God the Father] worked in Christ when he raised him from the dead and seated him at his right hand in the heavenly places, far above all rule and authority and power and dominion, and above every name that is named, not only in this age but also in the one to come" (Eph. 1:20–21 ESV). The author of the book of Hebrews writes, "After he had provided purification for sins, he sat down at the right hand of the Majesty in heaven" (1:3). His redemptive sacrifice was complete, as was his time on earth in incarnate form.

He Would Receive the Heavenly Honor Due to Him

Do you recall Christ's High Priestly Prayer just before his arrest: "Father, glorify me in your presence with the glory I had with you before the world began" (John 17:5)? Christ's return to the Father meant a return to the glory that had been his. The words of another text confirm that "God exalted him to the highest place and gave him the name that is above every name" (Phil. 2:9).

He Would Prepare a Place

On the night of the Last Supper with his disciples, Christ promised, "If I go and prepare a place for you, I will come back and take you to be with me that you also may be where I am" (John 14:3). Christ's ascension was necessary in order for him to undertake his plans to prepare for our life in heaven with the triune God.

The Ascension Touches Our Lives

The ascension also has implications for us who are Christ's worshippers. Some important guarantees flow from the ascension and have personal application to all believers.

The Ascension Guarantees Our Future Ascension

Since we are united with Christ, his return to heaven foreshadows our future ascension through the veil into heaven with him (see Heb. 10:20). Meanwhile, by faith we are seated in the heavenlies now until Christ's physical return. Remember these words of promise? "We who are still alive and are left will be caught up together with them in the clouds to meet the Lord in the air. And so we will be with the Lord forever" (1 Thess. 4:17). What a glorious promise to hold onto! In another letter, the apostle Paul encourages believers,

> Since, then, you have been raised with Christ, set your hearts on things above, where Christ is, seated at the right hand of God. . . . When Christ, who is your life, appears, then you also will appear with him in glory. (Col. 3:1, 4)

The Ascension Guarantees Our Advocate in Heaven

The apostle writes to his friends in Rome that Christ is "at the right hand of God and is also interceding for us" (Rom. 8:34). The writer to the Hebrews corroborates this with these words of assurance: "He is able to save completely those who come to God through him, because he always lives to intercede for them" (7:25). Knowing that Christ intercedes for us in prayer has implications for both our private prayers and also the prayers that we offer when we assemble for corporate worship. You might find it a powerful incentive to keep your mind from wandering during times of corporate prayer if you let this truth really sink in.

The Ascension Guarantees Christ's Presence with Us

Christ continues to be present with us—not physically, as he was during the incarnation, but in a new spiritual way through his indwelling Holy Spirit. Christ's ascension was necessary for the coming of the Holy Spirit. In the words of the famous Heidelberg Catechism, "Christ is true man and true God. With respect to His human nature He is no longer on earth, but with respect to His divinity, majesty, grace, and Spirit He is never absent from us."[7]

---

7. Heidelberg Catechism, answer 47.

The ascension brought about not Christ's physical remoteness but rather his spiritual nearness. One of his final sayings before his ascension, which is recorded at the end of Matthew, was this: "Surely I am with you always, to the very end of the age" (28:20). I love the way that the Reformer John Calvin expresses this truth: "Christ left us in such a way that his presence might be more useful to us—a presence that had been confined in a humble abode of flesh so long as he sojourned on earth."[8] And as theologian Gregg Allison explains, "After the ascension, this more 'useful' presence is none other the Holy Spirit."[9]

The Ascension Motivates Us to Worship Christ

We have seen that worship was the disciples' immediate response on the mountain, and then, as they returned to the temple, they continued to worship as they awaited the day of Pentecost: "They worshiped him and returned to Jerusalem with great joy. And they stayed continually at the temple, praising God" (Luke 24:52–53). Notice how this emphasis on worship at the end of Luke's gospel forms a symmetry with how it begins—worship bookends Luke's gospel. The book opens with Zechariah being engaged in his priestly duties of worship in the temple and with Simeon, who breaks forth in a hymn of adoration and worship upon seeing the infant Jesus (see 1:8–25; 2:22–35). Twenty-four chapters later, the book concludes on the same note of adoration.

Bible teacher and author Charles Swindoll provides this insight: "Luke's concluding summary statement uses the imperfect tense, showing ongoing action. The followers of Jesus 'were

8. John T. McNeill, ed., *Calvin: Institutes of the Christian Religion*, trans. Ford Lewis Battles, vol. 1 (1960; repr., Louisville: Westminster John Knox Press, 2006), 2.16.14.

9. Gregg R. Allison, *Historical Theology: An Introduction to Christian Doctrine* (Grand Rapids: Zondervan, 2011), 419.

continually in the temple praising God.' The heart of darkness had been taken back. Soon the Holy Spirit would fall like lightning on the followers of Christ, and the light of the gospel would emanate from God's holy hill."[10]

The Ascension Guarantees Christ's Return

Christ's earthly departure causes us to joyfully anticipate his return. When we move to the next and final mountain, the heavenly Mount Zion in Hebrews 12, we'll see how this all fits into place for those of us who live in this age of overlap between the ascension and the second coming of Christ.

Skyscrapers

The term *skyscraper* was first used in the 1880s to describe a multistory building—one that ranged from ten to twenty floors. Today the designation is often used for buildings that have a minimum of forty to fifty floors. But I'd like to use skyscrapers in a metaphorical sense to explain what we're doing with each successive narrative in this book. Scripture can be compared to a skyscraper—each of its narrative components builds on another to form a larger story, just as the individual floors of a skyscraper build on the others. I'm sure you have caught that progression as we've worked our way through Scripture from one chapter to another in this book. Hopefully, in the pages of the next chapter, you will gain an increased appreciation for how all the stories build on each other within the unifying metaphor of the divine presence—the *Coram Deo*.

Mountain seven is calling us!

---

10. Charles R. Swindoll, *Insights on Luke*, Swindoll's New Testament Insights (Grand Rapids: Zondervan, 2012), 526.

Questions for Reflection and Discussion

1. Look at the chart in this chapter that shows seven dimensions of God's presence. Explain in your own words what you think these dimensions mean. Does this raise any questions in your mind?
2. Why do you think the Mount of Olives might have been chosen for Christ's ascension?
3. Describe the impact that the ascension had on the disciples. Why did they respond the way they did?
4. What is meant by the "session" of Christ?
5. What does the ascension guarantee for us who worship and follow Christ?
6. Should Christians devote attention to observing Ascension Day? If so, how might the church celebrate it?
7. Can you name the six mountains we have considered so far? What common threads do you see between them? Are there any additional mountain scenes in Scripture that stand out in your mind?

11

ULTIMATE DESTINATION

Mount Zion Above: Mountain
of Heavenly Worship

Even the architecture of the heavenly city highlights the goal
of divine nearness. The throne of God and the Lamb, the
location of God's presence to govern his kingdom, is the center
of the city. Likewise, the river of life—another symbol of divine
nearness—flows from the royal throne of God's presence.
—J. Ryan Lister, *The Presence of God*

Even in our current culture, the idea of heaven cannot be easily dismissed. Despite the earnest attempts of those who want to suppress it, the subject keeps popping up—sometimes when you least expect it. Recently I turned on my television in time to catch a commercial for a popular vacation resort company that offered luxurious properties in exotic tropical locations and showed romantic white powder beaches and too-beautiful-to-be-real guests. A seductive voice promised, "Visit this resort, and you'll be as close to heaven as it is possible on earth!" Sound irresistible? By the time you finish this chapter, I trust that you'll appreciate a better way to get a taste of heaven.

In this final chapter, we move from earthly mountains into a new dimension of heavenly worship. As was first evident in the garden of Eden, God designed from the beginning for his presence to dwell among us. All redemptive history leads us to the eternal experience of enjoying his presence in the new heaven and earth. The Snake Crusher leads us back to the garden in the book of Revelation.[1] Now, in this chapter, we have finally arrived at that ultimate destination—the seventh summit.

At the beginning of chapter 1, I told the dubiously humorous story about a young boy who feared that he might be bored to death in a worship service. I lamented the fact that all too many adults share the same sentiment each Sunday. On this subject, the forceful preacher A. W. Tozer did not mince words: "I can safely say, on the authority of all that is revealed in the Word of God, that any man or woman on this earth who is bored and turned off by worship is not ready for heaven."[2] Tozer's no-nonsense assessment is sobering. The truth is that worship in heaven and on earth are inseparably linked. We will delve into that linkage in three dimensions of time: past, future, and present. This will require some stretching.

Past Worship: A Shadow of Heavenly Worship

The Old Testament contains numerous examples of the linkage between earthly worship and the heavenly angels. Angels are usually presented as invisible, bodiless beings that are devoted to the worship of God and that sometimes move between our present visible world and the dimension of heaven. For example, at the Mount Sinai prototype assembly, the earthly worshippers

1. Some readers may recognize this expression about the Snake Crusher from the subtitle of Kevin DeYoung's book *The Biggest Story: How the Snake Crusher Brings Us Back to the Garden* (Wheaton, IL: Crossway, 2015).

2. Kevin P. Emmert, ed., *Worship: The Reason We Were Created—Collected Insights from A. W. Tozer* (Chicago: Moody, 2017), 13.

assembled at the base of the mountain as the heavenly angels circled above: "The LORD came from Sinai and dawned over them from Seir; he shone forth from Mount Paran. He came with myriads [ten thousand] of holy ones from the south, from his mountain slopes" (Deut. 33:2). Those ten thousand holy ones were angelic heavenly beings who joined God on the mountain.

Perhaps the most compelling Old Testament example that illustrates how heavenly and earthly worship are connected is a familiar story from the life of the patriarch Jacob. Jacob was in flight, hoping to escape the well-deserved wrath of his elder brother, Esau, whom he had tricked out of his rightful claim to blessing as the firstborn. When the sun began to set, Jacob stopped for the night in the hill country at a place called Bethel (House of God), somewhere on the road between Beersheba and Haran, not far from Jerusalem. In ancient times, it was common for people to sleep on metal headrests, so perhaps the hard stone that Jacob used that night as a pillow did not cause him unusual discomfort.

But what he experienced that night as he slept under the roof of the sky was unlike anything that any human had experienced before. Jacob saw angelic beings moving between heaven and earth. In a divinely invoked dream, "he saw a stairway resting on the earth, with its top reaching to heaven, and the angels of God were ascending and descending on it. There above it stood the LORD" (Gen. 28:12–13). For a short time, the veil that separated the visible from the invisible was lifted, allowing Jacob a glimpse into the dimension that is normally invisible to humans. No wonder that when Jacob awoke he was gripped with fear and uttered these words: "Surely the LORD is in this place, and I was not aware of it. . . . How awesome is this place! This is none other than the house of God; this is the gate of heaven" (vv. 16–17).[3]

3. "Jacob's vision may have inspired more works of art than any other dream in history. Everything from Chagall's painting of a simple wooden ladder to William Blake's illustration of an elegant spiral staircase has been used in an attempt to

From the New Testament book of Hebrews, we learn that a further connection existed between the tabernacle and heaven. The author of Hebrews makes this evident when he describes the tabernacle as "a copy and shadow of what is in heaven" (8:5). The sacrificial system that was used in the tabernacle included "copies of the heavenly things" (9:23), which refers to the furnishings.

To enter the tabernacle was to experience a foretaste of heaven on earth. The high priest who went behind the curtain into the Most Holy Place on the Day of Atonement was reminded of the angelic presence by the two golden cherubim who stood with outstretched wings above the ark of the covenant. Other members of the Levitical priesthood were reminded of the angelic presence by the skillfully woven designs of angelic beings in the curtains that were used in temple and tabernacle worship. The inside of the tabernacle was decorated with curtains that were made from blue, purple, and scarlet yarns woven with airborne cherubim. The thick veil that separated the Holy Place from the holy of holies also included angelic cherubim that were woven into the fabric. This brought to mind the cherubim that guarded the entrance to the garden of Eden as well as the angelic host who fill the heavenly dimension. Thus the tabernacle reflected in a visible way the invisible reality of heaven.

As we learned in chapter 5, the temple on Mount Zion also illustrated the linkage between heaven and earth. It was constructed, per God's specifications, in a similar way to the pattern that had been used in the tabernacle. It, too, became a type and shadow of the heavenly sanctuary. As Edmund Jacob explains, "There was no image of God in the temple, but certain architectural features such as the palm trees and the cherubim constituted

capture the essence of the scene." Matthew Sleeth, *Reforesting Faith: What Trees Teach Us About the Nature of God and His Love for Us* (Colorado Springs: WaterBrook, 2019), 57.

a reminder of paradise and gave to the faithful a foretaste of what he hoped to see established."[4]

There is no shortage of evidence to support the linkage between heavenly and earthly worship that existed under the Old Covenant. But what will worship be like in the future?

Future Worship: The Eternal Consummation of Our Created Purpose

You and I were created to enjoy the presence of God— to dwell with him eternally. His plan is to unite us in heavenly worship at the return of Christ. This gathering at Christ's second coming is described in a series of three Greek terms from the New Testament.

- *Episunagogues*: The apostle Paul uses this word to describe Christ's second coming when he writes, "Our being *gathered* to him" (2 Thess. 2:1).

- *Episunagogousin*: Christ uses the cognate verb for "gather" to describe what will happen at his return. "He will send his angels with a loud trumpet call, and they will *gather* his elect from the four winds, from one end of the heavens to the other" (Matt. 24:31).

- *Episunagogen*: The noun form of the verb for "gather" is used to describe our present earthly worship assemblies. Hebrews 10:25 warns us not to "[give] up *meeting together* . . . and all the more as you see the Day approaching."

That approaching Day is the day of Christ's promised return. It is that anticipated assembly at his return that gives meaning

4. Edmond Jacob, *Theology of the Old Testament* (New York: Harper and Rowe, 1958), 259.

to our present preparatory assemblies on the Lord's Day. Pastors have every reason to be concerned about members of their flock who are casual about church attendance and who view it not as an appointment to meet with God but as something more like rental car insurance—optional. With few exceptions, listening to a podcast or viewing a telecast is not an acceptable substitute for gathering with God's people for corporate worship. Regular church attendance should be given top priority in the Sunday schedule of every believer who is physically able, as preparation for the ultimate assembly that is yet to come.

Depictions of the Consummation

The dimensions of the consummation that will be ushered in at Christ's return are difficult for us to grasp in our present earthly state, but God has given us clues in the book of Revelation. Artists and musicians throughout history have been inspired to create works that echo the teaching of Revelation.

One of my favorite artists, Jan van Eyck (ca. 1390–1441), attempted to portray the splendor of heavenly worship that is described in Revelation 5 in his *Adoration of the Lamb*, which is the center panel of his altarpiece in the Cathedral of Saint Bavo in Ghent, Belgium. This classic work of art came to the public's attention again in the early twenty-first century through the release of the movie *The Monuments Men*, which portrayed the story of the Nazis' theft of this valuable art treasure during World War II.

The primary focus of Van Eyck's center panel is the Lamb, who is portrayed as slain and yet still alive, standing on a crimson altar. His lifeblood flows from his throat into a chalice—an image that is based on Revelation 5:6, "I saw a Lamb, looking as if it had been slain, standing at the center of the throne." Heavenly angels surround the Lamb's throne, each of them carrying objects that are related to the crucifixion of Christ. One angel carries the cross, another the crown of thorns. Another angel carries the sword that

Fig. 11.1. Van Eyck's *Adoration of the Lamb*

pierced Christ's side. Van Eyck also portrays an angel who carries the pole on which someone placed the sponge of vinegar that assuaged Christ's thirst.

The Ghent altarpiece includes 330 heads, no two of which are alike. The outer groups consist of people from all classes and types—men and women, rich and poor—all of whom have come to adore the Lamb. The worshippers include the apostles, the virgin martyrs, twelve Old Testament prophets, and others from the Old Testament who anticipated the arrival of the Lamb. At the top center of the masterpiece, Van Eyck has painted the sun, within which we see a dove—emblematic of the presence of God's Holy Spirit. The sunshine and dove emit linear rays of light that stream downward, reminding us that both human and angelic creatures are able, through the Spirit's work, to worship the Lamb in Spirit and in truth.

This Van Eyck painting is one of the world's treasures, but it's also so much more. It should incite us to join the procession of worshippers who will one day kneel before the Lamb and cry out,

"You are worthy." It should evoke in us an overwhelming sense of anticipation to personally participate in that future heavenly scene.

Glimpse of Heavenly Worship in Revelation 5

Our anticipation of and longing for heaven can also be awakened through a closer look at the future consummated heavenly worship that is described in the book of Revelation. The apostle explains how an angel of God "carried me away in the Spirit to a mountain great and high, and showed me the Holy City, Jerusalem, coming down out of heaven from God" (Rev. 21:10). The book of Revelation contains multiple scenes of future heavenly worship. For example, in Revelation 5, John gives us a glimpse of the heavenly drama and glorious worship that awaits believers, who will one day be caught up in what can only be described as rapturous joy. What can we foresee about heavenly worship?

Heavenly worship is Lamb-centered. Christ is the focal point of this worship, because he alone is worthy to open the scroll as the omnipotent and omniscient one. Scripture employs the strange zoological juxtaposition of a lion and a lamb in the heavenly kingdom. This calls to mind an incident in C. S. Lewis's Narnia tale *The Voyage of the Dawn Treader* in which the Pevensie children encounter a lamb at the World's End. The lamb's "snowy white flushed into tawny gold and his size changed," and he becomes the lion Aslan, "towering above them and scattering light from his mane."[5] In Lewis's story, a lamb turns into a lion, whereas the opposite occurs in John's vision that's recorded in Revelation. John is told that a lion will open the scroll, but a Lamb mysteriously appears. Only he is worthy to open the scroll and reveal the future.

The Lamb in John's vision is also worthy of our worship

---

5. C. S. Lewis, *The Voyage of the* Dawn Treader (repr., New York: HarperCollins, 1994), 215.

because he is coequal with the Father and has redeemed us from our sin by shedding his lifeblood. The root of the Greek word that is translated into English as "slain" in verse 6 conveys the idea of "having the throat cut." This redemptive role of the Lamb reinforces what we have learned earlier in this book—our worship should have a Christocentric focus.

Heavenly worship vibrates with songs of praise. The English lyric poet Christina Rossetti described heaven as "the home-land of music."[6] But what do we know about the music of heaven? We are told in Scripture that the heavenly songs are "new" songs of praise. Perhaps they are new because in heaven Christ opens up the new consummated era of his redemptive plan. Perhaps it is also because the Lord continues to perform new acts of mercy. It would be impossible to exhaust the new things that the Lord has done and for which we can create new songs.

Notice also how the heavenly songs are God-centered rather than man-centered. For example, in Revelation 5:12 a sevenfold ascription of praise piles word upon word upon word in adoration of Christ: "Worthy is the Lamb that was slain to receive power and riches and wisdom and might and honor and glory and blessing" (NASB). In John's day, when the Roman emperor appeared before his subjects, they would honor him by chanting, "You are worthy" (*vere dingus*). In contrast, John indicates that only the Lamb is worthy. This is the reality that is celebrated in heavenly music. The important conclusion that we can draw is this: our present earthly worship should prepare us for heavenly worship by teaching us to appreciate God-centered songs of praise—songs that focus on the attributes and acts of the triune God.

We can also conclude that the songs of heaven are dynamic

---

6. Christina G. Rossetti, *The Face of the Deep: A Devotional Commentary on the Apocalypse* (London, 1892), 352.

and multilayered, as they expand outward from the center of the throne in waves of worship and praise. The singing described in Revelation 5 begins with the twenty-four elders in the first circle surrounding the throne. They are joined by angels who form a second circle that numbers ten thousand times ten thousand and thousands of thousands. Beyond this company is a third group of worshippers that is described in verse 13: "Then I heard every creature in heaven and on earth and under the earth and on the sea, and all that is in them, saying: 'To him who sits on the throne and to the Lamb be praise and honor and glory and power, for ever and ever!'" No wonder the elders in that heavenly scene fell down and worshipped. Yes, music is intrinsic to heavenly worship—a reality that we can anticipate and prepare for with our selection of music each Lord's Day.

Present Worship: Participation in Heavenly Worship through Christ by Faith

How does all this talk about the connection between past and future worship relate to our present worship?

All believers can now participate in heavenly realities through the person of Christ—the fulfiller of the forms and ceremonies of the Old Testament. We learn this in the context of Jesus's calling his earliest disciples to follow him. One of these disciples, Nathanael, initially approached Jesus with skepticism. Their ensuing conversation culminated with Christ speaking these prophetic words to Nathanael: "Very truly I tell you, you will see 'heaven open, and the angels of God ascending and descending on' the Son of Man" (John 1:51). Jesus's choice of imagery references Jacob's dream. Jesus revealed that he himself replaces the ladder between earth and heaven. Jesus, as the fulfillment of Jacob's ladder, becomes the means of traversing the gap between the two dimensions of earth and heaven.

Handel's Glimpse of Heaven

What Van Eyck attempted to portray on canvas, the composer George Frideric Handel undertook to express musically in his famous oratorio *Messiah*. If you have the opportunity to attend, or better yet sing in, one of the many seasonal performances of this oratorio that take place around the world each year, you will likely, after well over an hour of glorious music, hear the oratorio reach a soul-stirring crescendo with the heavenly chorus "Worthy is the Lamb," which is based on our text in Revelation 5. You may have heard that when Handel completed composing this music, he firmly penned, at the end of the 259-page score, the initials SDG, for "Soli Deo Gloria"—to God alone the glory.

The story is told that at one point, after Handel had remained alone in his room for an inordinate amount of time composing this oratorio, his fretful servant decided to check on him. Upon entering Handel's room, he found the great composer dissolved in tears. When asked the reason for his weeping, Handel replied, "I did think that I did see all Heaven before me, and the great God Himself!" Although the story may be apocryphal, Handel's tears of joy help us to appreciate that heavenly worship will be anything but boring.

It is not only through the *person* of Christ but also through the *work* of Christ that we can participate in heavenly realities. Scripture tells us that after Christ completed his high priestly work on the cross and rose from the dead, he ascended into the heavenlies on our behalf to enter the Most Holy Place above. This is the real sanctuary that had been visible in shadow form in the earthly tabernacle and temple. The author of Hebrews explains that Christ "sat down at the right hand of the throne of the Majesty in heaven" (8:1); "he entered heaven itself, now to appear for us in God's presence" (9:24). You and I now enjoy new access to the heavenly dimension. The barricade between heaven and earth has been torn down—never to be rebuilt.

We will have access to the heavenly dimension at our death, or at the second coming of Christ—whichever comes first. But what about now? Scripture assures us that we can now participate in heavenly realities through our worship as we ascend by faith to the heavenly Zion. The key words here are *by faith*. "God raised us up with Christ and seated us with him in heavenly realms in Christ Jesus" (Eph. 2:6). This describes not a future reality but something that's in place right now. The union of the earthly church militant with the heavenly church triumphant is a present, though imperfect, reality.[7]

Contrasting Mountains

One of the best texts in the entire New Testament that summarizes the biblical theology of worship is Hebrews 12:18–24. This text draws a clear contrast between the past and the present—between the earthly experience of worship on Mount Sinai and the experience of worship on Mount Zion, the heavenly city. Let's look at the contrasts.

Mount Sinai Fear (Heb. 12:18–21)

The past earthly worship at Mount Sinai can be characterized as an experience of sheer terror. This fright was fomented by the physical phenomena that are described in the Exodus account. Imagine standing at the foot of this massive mountain watching the flames shoot into the air, inhaling the smoke, shuddering at

---

7. By *the church militant*, I refer to believers on earth who are called to fight the good fight of faith. By the *church triumphant*, I refer to believers who have run the course and are now with the Lord. The militant and triumphant groups are one church. We are already united in a present real sense, though not in the final consummated sense. We experience this uniting reality most vividly when we assemble for corporate worship.

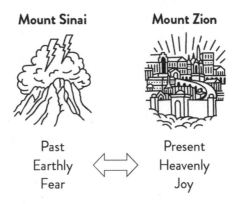

Mount Sinai   **Mount Zion**

Past   Present
Earthly   ⟺   Heavenly
Fear   Joy

Fig. 11.2. Contrast between Mounts Sinai and Zion

the bolts of lightning and claps of thunder, covering your ears at the deafening blast of the trumpet, feeling the very ground quake beneath your feet, and finally hearing the voice of God himself. This was not an ordinary adrenaline rush! The fear that God's people experienced at the foot of the mountain was exacerbated by their recognition that they were sinful mortals who were standing on holy ground in the very presence of God. The experience was so terrifying that even Moses quaked with fear.

Thankfully, when you and I enter God's holy presence in worship assemblies, we no longer need be consumed with fright. Generations after the Sinai assembly, Christ's blood was shed on the cross to remove the terror that was associated with worship.

Mount Zion Joy (Heb. 12:22–24)

Contrast the worship at Mount Sinai with the worship that is now possible for believers, by faith, at the heavenly Mount Zion. Our experience of worship today at the heavenly Mount Zion should evoke a sense of joy, not terror. Hebrews 12:22–24 explains our reasons for joy.

Each Lord's Day, you and I are invited to climb Mount Zion, in the heavenly Jerusalem, and to spiritually participate in invisible

197

realities. Our feet may be planted on earth when we enter our places of worship, but our spirits can soar by faith as we join the ascended Christ around the throne. The location for our worship is no longer Mount Sinai or even the earthly Mount Zion. Christians do not have to wait until death, or even the second coming of Christ, to experience a foretaste of that joyful heavenly assembly.

Over the years, I have had the opportunity, while sitting on the platform at the front of many church sanctuaries, to observe the people in the congregation as they gather to worship and hustle to their seats in the minutes before the service begins. Most are preoccupied with locating family members and friends or with engaging in a quick conversation before the service. But Hebrews 12 reminds us that unseen, invisible, heavenly companions are also present in our assemblies. This should evoke joy—and maybe even send a shiver up our spine!

We don't have to guess their identity. They are named in verses 22–23: thousands of angels in joyful assembly, the church of the firstborn (which likely means elect saints of the past who are part of the cloud of eyewitnesses—including loved ones who have already died in Christ), and God himself. How do we know that God is present? Because the text indicates that "you have come to God... to Jesus" (vv. 23–24). The word that is translated as "come" has reverential overtones, implying that this is not an ordinary coming to anywhere for any reason, but a coming for the purpose of worship.

I find it helpful when I'm attending a worship service to remind myself of these biblical truths. "There's more going on than meets the eye. Don't forget the invisible dimension. Remember who's watching and listening."

Reflecting the Heaven/Earth Linkage in Our Churches

How can the linkage between heavenly and earthly worship be reflected today in our worship services?

Through prayer. Our prayers enable us to approach the heavenly throne. Each time that we pray the Lord's Prayer, we reflect this linkage. Note the words "Our Father in heaven . . . your kingdom come . . . on earth as it is in heaven." This prayer's connection with heaven is reflected in a prayer that's found in *The Book of Common Prayer*: "We praise you, joining our voices with Angels and Archangels and with all the company of heaven, who for ever sing this hymn to proclaim the glory of your Name."[8]

Through the Lord's Supper. The Lord's Supper has a heavenly flavor. Each time that we gather around the table, we can anticipate the heavenly supper at Christ's return (see Matt. 26:20; 1 Cor. 11:26; Rev. 19:9).

Through our praise. Our present songs of praise, though they are sung on earth, are a form of participation in the heavenly praise that is now being sung unceasingly around the throne. As you and I sing to the Lord, our songs blend with those of the angelic hosts. A clear example of this heavenly link is the traditional doxology that refers to both earth and heaven being joined: "creatures here below" as well as, "above, ye heavenly hosts." A number of hymns and songs reflect the truth of this heavenly linkage. Learning to listen for these references during services will add richness to your worship.

Concluding Thoughts

In my travels over the years, I have had the opportunity to visit and tour churches from a variety of Eastern traditions in many parts of the world. One of the distinctive features of the architecture of these churches is a domed ceiling that is painted

8. *The Book of Common Prayer* (New York: Seabury Press, 1979), 362.

with icons of angels and the hosts of heaven. These represent the angelic hosts who are spiritually present and who hover over the heads of those who are gathered in worship on the floor below. This architecture is designed to bring heaven down to earth and to transport earth to heaven.

A striking illustration of this is seen in the original structure of one of my favorite churches: Hagia Sophia, the Church of Divine Wisdom, in Istanbul, Turkey. When it was originally built, it was the world's largest church. One hundred master builders supervised ten thousand workers until its completion in AD 360. After a destructive fire in AD 532, Justinian, the Byzantine Emperor, arranged to have it rebuilt. When Hagia Sophia reopened in AD 537, Justinian entered the completed building and exclaimed, "Solomon, I have surpassed you."

Supposedly, around AD 988, Vladimir, the Russian prince of Kiev, sent out emissaries to search for the true religion so that he could unite his people under one church. His emissaries visited Muslims, Roman Catholic Christians in western Europe, and followers of Judaism. Finally, they traveled to Constantinople and made their way to Hagia Sophia. Vladimir's emissaries tarried for some time in the sanctuary, deeply stirred by the worship. The emotional impact of the experience was so intense that they reported back to the Russian prince, "We knew not whether we were in heaven or on earth, for surely there is no such splendor or beauty anywhere upon earth. We cannot describe it to you; only this we know, that God dwells there among men, and that their service surpasses the worship of all other places."[9]

I have often reflected on this story and on its implications for today's church. Is what the emissaries reported back to Vladimir descriptive of what people experience in a typical service of

9. Quoted in Timothy Ware, *The Orthodox Church* (Baltimore: Penguin, 1963), 269, quoted in Robert E. Webber, *Worship Old and New* (Grand Rapids: Zondervan, 1994), 65.

worship in your church? How many visitors who attend your church could honestly say, "We did not know if we were in heaven or on earth. We feel like we've been to heaven"? How many churches can report what the apostle Paul tells us can happen when an unbeliever or inquirer comes into the church: "They will fall down and worship God, exclaiming, 'God is really among you!'" (1 Cor 14:25)?

We have seen that the unifying metaphor that describes worship assemblies throughout both Old and New Testament history

---

Welcome to the Celestial City

John Bunyan, in his allegorical classic *Pilgrim's Progress*, uses his imagination to describe what Christian's entry into the celestial city was like. Here's an adapted, contemporary version of his description.

Slowly the great, shining doors opened and the pilgrims saw inside the heavenly city for the first time. One glance, and they were changed men. Their faces shone, their eyes sparkled, and they stepped eagerly forward, past the gate and into the golden streets. And what a welcome they received! The city's bells pealed, and the inhabitants of heaven, who had gathered to meet them, pressed round, smiling and calling out greetings or singing and making music for the new arrivals. They also gave them golden clothes, crowns and harps. Christian and Hopeful could stay silent no longer. The words burst from them: "Hallelujah! Praise to our Prince and King for ever and ever!" Then the gates closed behind them, and they knew they were safely home at last.*

*Jean Watson, ed., *The Family Pilgrim's Progress: From the Original Story by John Bunyan* (Wheaton, IL: Tyndale House, 1983), 126.

---

is the presence of God—God's promise to dwell among us. It's a promise that came to fulfillment in Christ's incarnation and will come to permanent fullness one day in the future when Christ returns. Edenic perfection and communion will be restored in the new heaven and earth. Until then, we pray, "Even so, come Lord Jesus!"

Every Chapter Is Better

I'd like to conclude this book by quoting the words of Lewis from the final page of the final chapter of the final Narnia book, *The Last Battle*.

And as [Aslan] spoke He no longer looked to them like a lion; but the things that began to happen after that were so great and beautiful that I cannot write them. And for us this is the end of all the stories, and we can most truly say that they all lived happily ever after. But for them it was only the beginning of the real Story. All their life in this world and all their adventures in Narnia had only been the cover and the title page: now at last they were beginning Chapter One of the Great Story which no one on earth has read, which goes on forever, in which every chapter is better than the one before.[10]

Amen.

Questions for Reflection and Discussion

1. What is meant by saying that the Snake Crusher leads us back to the garden?

10. C. S. Lewis, *The Last Battle*, in *The Chronicles of Narnia* (New York: HarperCollins, 2004), 767.

2. Tozer wrote, "Any man or woman on this earth who is bored and turned off by worship is not ready for heaven." What do you think he might have meant? Do you agree or disagree with this statement? Why?

3. Explain the linkage between earth and heaven in Old Testament worship.

4. Look at Revelation 5:6–14. Summarize what it teaches us about heavenly worship. How does this apply to our worship today?

5. Read Hebrews 12:18–24 and summarize in your own words what is occurring in our present worship.

6. Describe some ways that we can reflect the heaven/earth linkage in our present corporate worship services. How is your church doing in this area?

7. As a result of reading this book, what are some changes you might like to make in your thinking, understanding, and practices of worship?[11]

---

11. See the appendix, "Suggestions for Preparing to Attend Sunday Worship."

APPENDIX

Suggestions for Preparing to Attend Sunday Worship

Acceptable worship does not happen spontaneously.
Preparation is essential. In a worship service, for example,
the choir prepares, the preacher prepares, and the organist
and other musicians prepare. But the most important
preparation of all is the preparation of the individual
worshiper, and that is usually the most neglected.
—John MacArthur Jr., *The Ultimate Priority*

The following seven suggestions summarize some of the ways in which you might prepare for assemblies of Sunday worship. These are recommendations to help you avoid the danger of attending a church service and yet missing worship. May Sunday worship be the highlight of your week!

1. Confess

Scripture reminds us to confess our sins before approaching God in worship.

Who may ascend the mountain of the LORD?
  Who may stand in his holy place?
The one who has clean hands and a pure heart,
  who does not trust in an idol
  or swear by a false god. (Ps. 24:3–4)

Some churches include a prayer of confession as part of the order of service. But whether this is included in it or not, we can also individually confess our sins prior to going to the service or while waiting during the minutes before it begins.

2. Reconcile

Significant interpersonal conflicts should be resolved so that our worship will not be impeded. "If you are offering your gift at the altar and there remember that your brother or sister has something against you, leave your gift there in front of the altar. First go and be reconciled to them; then come and offer your gift" (Matt. 5:23–24).

3. Preread

If your church publishes the order of service in advance, look up the listed Scripture texts and prayerfully read them before coming. Or you may read from the Psalms of Ascent (Pss. 120–34), which God's people used when approaching the temple in Jerusalem. You might also read through the lyrics of the hymns or songs in the service, if they are published in advance.

4. Adore

In your private worship during the week, focus on a single act or attribute of God that may relate to the approaching church service. Examples include God's acts of creation or redemption and his attributes of omnipotence or faithfulness. Read a chapter on the same topic in classics such as A. W. Tozer's *Knowledge of the Holy*, J. I. Packer's *Knowing God*, A. W. Pink's *Attributes of God*, or the more recent *God Is: A Devotional Guide to the Attributes of God* by Mark Jones. These can add biblical fuel to spark your worship.[1]

5. Recall

Before the service begins, or even during pauses in it, remind yourself of some of the biblical and theological truths that were taught in this book—especially the reality of God's plan for his presence to dwell with us as we worship him in spirit and truth. You might even copy some quotes from the book onto your phone's memo app to read as a reminder.

6. Expect

Come expecting to be an active participant rather than a passive spectator. Expect that you will meet with God and will exercise your priesthood to engage in whole-person adoration.

7. Pray

Take time to pray, in advance of your church's worship service, for the individuals who plan and lead it. Ask that the Spirit of the Lord will fill and guide them in such a way that the presence of God might be recognized by those who enter the assemblies of your church.

---

1. See "Suggestions for Further Reading" for more titles.

*Father, my soul longs to enter more fully into the awesome
and majestic reality of worship. But to die to self and be lost in
worshipping you is easier said than done. I confess that I have not
been preoccupied with you as I ought to be and that my preparation
for Sunday worship has been negligible. I well know that my
highest duty and privilege in this life and the next is to worship
my Creator. Grant me a worshipping heart, O God, that I might
encounter you in all your glory. This I pray in the name of the One
who alone is worthy of my worship through Christ. Amen.*

SUGGESTIONS FOR FURTHER READING

Alexander, T. Desmond. *The City of God and the Goal of Creation.* Wheaton, IL: Crossway, 2018.

————. *From Eden to the New Jerusalem: An Introduction to Biblical Theology.* 2008. Reprint, Grand Rapids: Kregel Academic, 2009.

Barrs, Jerram. *Echoes of Eden: Reflections on Christianity, Literature, and the Arts.* Wheaton, IL: Crossway, 2013.

Beale, G. K., and Mitchell Kim. *God Dwells among Us: Expanding Eden to the Ends of the Earth.* Downers Grove, IL: InterVarsity Press, 2014.

Block, Daniel I. *For the Glory of God: Recovering a Biblical Theology of Worship.* Grand Rapids: Baker Academic, 2014.

Emmert, Kevin P., ed. *Worship: The Reason We Were Created—Collected Insights from A. W. Tozer.* Chicago: Moody, 2017.

Frame, John M. *Worship in Spirit and Truth: A Refreshing Study of the Principles and Practice of Biblical Worship.* Phillipsburg, NJ: P&R, 1996.

Gibson, Jonathan, and Mark Earngey, eds. *Reformation Worship: Liturgies from the Past for the Present.* Greensboro, NC: New Growth Press, 2018.

Hays, J. Daniel. *The Temple and the Tabernacle: A Study of God's*

Dwelling Places from Genesis to Revelation. Grand Rapids: Baker Books, 2016.

Hyde, Daniel R. *God in Our Midst: The Tabernacle and Our Relationship with God*. Sanford, FL: Reformation Trust Publishing, 2012.

Lewis, C. S. *The Last Battle*. New York: Macmillan, 1956.

Lister, J. Ryan. *The Presence of God: Its Place in the Storyline of Scripture and the Story of Our Lives*. Wheaton, IL: Crossway, 2015.

Master, Jonathan L., ed. *The God We Worship: Adoring the One Who Pursues, Redeems, and Changes His People*. Phillipsburg, NJ: P&R, 2016.

Morales, L. Michael. *Who Shall Ascend the Mountain of the Lord? A Biblical Theology of the Book of Leviticus*. Downers Grove, IL: InterVarsity Press, 2015.

Morgan, Christopher W., and Robert A. Peterson, eds. *The Glory of God*. Theology in Community. Wheaton, IL: Crossway, 2010.

Nicholls, William. *Jacob's Ladder: The Meaning of Worship*. 1958. Reprint, Richmond: John Knox Press, 1963.

Poythress, Vern S. *Theophany: A Biblical Theology of God's Appearing*. Wheaton, IL: Crossway, 2018.

Schakel, Peter J. *Is Your Lord Large Enough? How C. S. Lewis Expands Our View of God*. Downers Grove, IL: IVP Books, 2008.

Sproul, R.C. *A Taste of Heaven: Worship in the Light of Eternity*. Lake Mary, FL: Reformation Trust Publishing, 2006.

Paul E. Engle (MDiv, Wheaton College Graduate School; DMin, Westminster Theological Seminary) is an ordained minister who has pastored churches in Pennsylvania, Connecticut, Illinois, and Michigan. He has also served as a visiting instructor at Trinity Evangelical Divinity School, New Geneva Theological Seminary, Knox Theological Seminary, Reformed Theological Seminary, and Dallas Theological Seminary. He teaches church leaders in the Philippines, Romania, Uganda, Cuba, Israel, and East Asia. He is the author of nine books, including *The Baker Wedding Handbook.* He and his wife live in Charlotte, North Carolina.

Did you find this book helpful?
Consider writing a review online.
The author appreciates your feedback!

Or write to P&R at editorial@prpbooks.com
with your comments. We'd love to hear from you.

Also from P&R Publishing

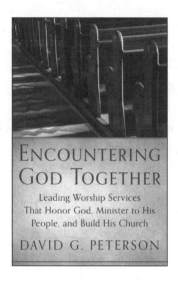

Have you experienced worship services that downplayed their focus on God's presence in order to emphasize fellowship and ministry? Or ones whose "worship" had little sense of believers' coming together to minister to one another? How do we regain the right balance in our services?

David Peterson will teach you:

- the biblical foundations of worship
- the meaning and purpose of gathering together
- patterns and varieties of service models

Discover how to structure each service so that you take worshipers on a meaningful journey together.

"Biblical, practical, and insightful guidelines for thinking through how God wants us to meet with him as we meet with each other. . . . *Encountering God Together* should be read by anyone involved in planning or leading gatherings of the church."
—**Bob Kauflin**, Director, Sovereign Grace Music